# Escape the Coming Night

## MESSAGES FROM
## THE BOOK OF REVELATION
### Volume 2

BY DR. DAVID JEREMIAH

# Turning Point

© 1994 by Turning Point Ministries
P.O. Box 3838
San Diego, CA 92163
All Rights Reserved

Published by Walk Thru the Bible Ministries, Atlanta, Georgia.

Unless otherwise indicated, the Scripture quotations in this study guide are from The New King James Version. Copyright ©1979, 1980, 1982, Thomas Nelson, Inc.

Printed in the United States of America.

# Contents

Dedication..........................................................................5

About Dr. David Jeremiah and Turning Point Ministries..........6

About This Study Guide....................................................7

Introduction.......................................................................9

1. A Look into Heaven (Revelation 4: 1-11)..........................11

2. Deed to the Earth (Revelation 5: 1-14)............................21

3. The Four Horsemen of the Apocalypse (Rev. 6: 1-8).........31

4. The Souls Under the Altar (Revelation 6: 9-11).................41

5. When the Whole World Trembles (Rev. 6: 12-17)..............51

6. Revival in the Tribulation (Revelation 7: 1-8)....................61

7. Tribulation Harvest (Revelation 7: 9-17)...........................71

8. The Seventh Seal (Revelation 8: 1-13)..............................81

9. The Fifth Trumpet—Hell on Earth Part 1 (Rev. 9: 1-12)......91

10. The Sixth Trumpet—Hell on Earth Part 2 (Rev. 9: 13-21) .101

11. Divine Parenthesis (Revelation 10: 1-11).........................111

12. The Two Witnesses (Revelation 11: 1-14).........................119

These study guides are lovingly dedicated to an incredible woman of the Word, Maxine Moore. Maxine listened to the audio teaching tapes on the Book of Revelation and wrote out each lesson by hand in order to teach these truths to the women in her weekly Bible study. At a Turning Point radio rally in Greensboro, North Carolina, she presented me with the final product of her year-long labor. She has been the inspiration behind these study guides. Thank you, Maxine, on behalf of all of us who will study Revelation with renewed interest.

David Jeremiah
San Diego, California
November 1993

# About Dr. David Jeremiah and Turning Point Ministries

Dr. David Jeremiah is the founder of Turning Point Ministries, a ministry committed to providing Christians with sound Bible teaching relevant to today's changing times through radio broadcasts, audiocassette series, and books. Dr. Jeremiah's "common sense" teaching on such topics as family, stress, the New Age, and Biblical prophecy forms the foundation of Turning Point Ministries.

Locating his home in San Diego, California, with wife Donna and four children, Dr. Jeremiah is the senior pastor of Shadow Mountain Community Church in El Cajon, where he also serves as president of Christian Heritage College.

In 1982, Dr. Jeremiah wanted to bring the same solid teaching to San Diego television that he shared weekly with his congregation. Shortly thereafter, Turning Point expanded its ministry to radio, and currently Dr. Jeremiah's inspiring messages are broadcast weekly from over 250 national and international radio stations.

Because Dr. Jeremiah desires to know his listening audience, he travels nationwide holding "A Night of Encouragement" radio rallies, which touch the hearts and lives of millions. According to Dr. Jeremiah:

"At some point in time, everyone reaches a turning point, and for every person, that moment is unique, an experience to hold onto forever. There's so much changing in today's world, sometimes it's difficult to always choose the right path. Turning Point Ministries offers real people an understanding of God's Word, as well as the opportunity to make a difference in their lives."

Dr. Jeremiah has also authored eight books, including *Escape the Coming Night*, which is based on the series of messages presented in this study guide.

# About This Study Guide

The purpose of this Turning Point study guide is to reinforce Dr. David Jeremiah's dynamic, in-depth teaching on the Book of Revelation and to aid the reader in applying Biblical truth to his or her daily life. This study guide is designed to be used in conjunction with Dr. Jeremiah's *Escape the Coming Night* audiocassette series, but it may also be used by itself for personal or group Bible study.

## Structure of the Lessons

Each lesson is based on one of the tapes in the *Escape the Coming Night* audiocassette series and focuses on a specific passage in the Book of Revelation. Each lesson is composed of the following elements:

## Outline

The outline at the beginning of the lesson gives a clear, concise picture of the passage being studied and provides a helpful framework for readers as they listen to Dr. Jeremiah's teaching.

## Overview

The overview summarizes Dr. Jeremiah's teaching on the passage being studied in the lesson. Readers should refer to the passage in their own Bibles as they study the overview.

## Application

This section contains a variety of questions designed to help readers dig deeper into the lesson and the Scriptures and to apply the lesson to their daily lives. For Bible study groups or Sunday school classes, these questions will provide a springboard for group discussion and interaction.

## Did You Know?

This section presents a fun fact, historical note, or insight which adds a point of interest to the preceding lesson.

## Using This Guide for Group Study

The lessons in this study guide are suitable for Sunday school classes, small-group studies, elective Bible studies, or home Bible study groups. Each person in the group should have his or her own study guide.

When possible, the study guide should be used with the corresponding tape series. You may wish to assign the study guide as homework prior to the meeting of the group, and then use the meeting time to listen to the tape and discuss the lesson.

## For Continuing Study

A complete catalog of Dr. Jeremiah's materials for personal and group study is available through Turning Point Ministries. To obtain a catalog, additional study guides, or more information about Turning Point, call 619-441-0225 or write to Turning Point Ministries, P.O. Box 3838, San Diego, CA 92163.

Dr. Jeremiah's "Turning Point" radio broadcast is currently heard on more than 250 national and international radio stations. Contact your local Christian radio station or Turning Point Ministries for program times in your area.

# Escape the Coming Night

In Revelation 1:19, we learn that the author John was called by God to "write the things which you have seen, and the things which are . . . ." Now begins the most in-depth and mysterious section of this book of Scripture, chapter 4, in which John focuses on "the things which will take place after this."

In this volume of Dr. David Jeremiah's messages from the Book of Revelation, twelve lessons focus on John's prophecies regarding the hereafter. Each lesson moves systematically through a small portion of Revelation 4-11, concluding in study questions that help you gain a personal grasp on the issues discussed.

## Where Is the Church?

What will occur in heaven while the Tribulation takes place on earth? This troubling question has a thrilling answer for Christians, who can anticipate worshiping the triune God on His throne in the beauty of His presence. Who the church is will also be explored.

In addition, discover what the scroll represents and who is worthy to unseal it. Then turn your eyes to the throne of God and find out who He is, and how He will be worshiped in His kingdom.

## The Tribulation Begins

Chapter 6 makes known God's wrath. Scrutinize the first four broken seals of the scrolls, which help to explain the events leading to the Tribulation. The Antichrist, war, famine, death, and hell are all prophesied. As we contemplate these horrors, the response of believers will become clear. The sorrow we feel for those who will suffer will spur us to intensified personal evangelism.

How great will be the suffering and persecution that occurs during the Tribulation? The answers to this question and others are found after the breaking of the fifth seal. Find out how God, in the midst of His greatest judgment, will still offer the mercy of salvation. Continue on and discover why God's great day of wrath finally occurs, what it entails, and how sinful men respond. Believers today will take heed to avoid sin and cling to God when the terrors of that awful day are revealed.

## Unexpected Encouragement

In the midst of tribulation and terror, God will occasion a great revival. When will this revival take place, and whom will it affect? Which of God's people will be sealed off from judgment and set apart from nonbelievers on earth? Who can explain the controversial references to "666" or to the "144,000"? You'll find encouragement in the answers to these questions and more.

## The Reign of Sin

The seventh and final seal is opened in Revelation 8, and the seven trumpet judgments are released. Lesson eight considers that time in the future when earth will become Satan's domain and man's sin will reign. Revelation 9 reminds us of the reality of an eternal hell, providing an important warning to men and women today.

## A Foretaste of Victory

Praise be to God that evil will not reign forever; ultimately, the King of heaven will be victorious. In Revelation 10, John receives a foretaste of that victory in a vision, which comes as relief from the tragedy of Tribulation. Another mercy is that during the Tribulation, God will send two witnesses to prophesy on His behalf. Who are they and what is their message?

## Before You Begin

As you study these lessons on the "hereafter," you may be shocked at the severity of God's judgment. Take time now to examine your life. If you do not trust Christ as Lord and Savior, the events in Revelation 4-11 will be your fate!

# A Look into Heaven

The church age has concluded. Now, everything and everyone are focused on the throne of God.

Something very dramatic has taken place between chapters 3 and 4, and the Rapture is the only possible explanation for the shift in emphasis. We will examine the reasons for this conclusion, and John's vision of heaven, with the throne as its focus of worship.

I. **Argument For the Rapture**
   A. Sequence of events in the Book of Revelation
   B. Silence in chapters 4-19 concerning the church
   C. Spirit of God's transfer from earth to heaven
   D. Symbolic presence of John in heaven

II. **Focus of Heaven** • the Throne of God
   A. Seated on it • the triune God
   B. Surrounding it • the rainbow
   C. Sitting around it • the 24 elders
   D. Spread before it • the sea of glass
   E. Situated in the midst of it • the four living creatures
   F. Singing praise to it • the angels and the church
      1. Object of their worship
      2. Method of their worship

When we last opened our Bibles to the Book of Revelation, our attention was focused on the church on the earth. The Laodicean church represents the church that will be on earth just before the return of Christ for His own. As we begin to read chapter 4, we discover that the church is no longer on the earth, but in heaven.

## The Rapture of the Church

Although the Rapture is not specifically mentioned in the Book of Revelation, it is clearly alluded to in this section of the book. It is the only possible explanation for the shift in emphasis. Let's examine the reasons for this argument.

## The Sequence of Events

The inspired outline of the Book of Revelation is given in Revelation 1:19. John was told to "write the things which you have seen." This refers to the vision of Christ which John saw, as recorded in 1:1-18. "And the things which are" include chapters 2 and 3, referring to the seven churches. This panoramic view of church history spans the time between the Day of Pentecost and the Rapture of the church. The third section of the book is designated as "the things which will take place after this" and encompasses chapters 4-22, the major section of the Book of Revelation. The happenings that begin in chapter 4 clearly take place after the church age is concluded. Therefore, the church is not involved in the things which are going on down here on the earth, as described in chapters 4-19.

## The Silence Regarding the Church

The word "church" appears 19 times in the first 3 chapters, but from Revelation 3:22 until chapter 19, it is not mentioned once as being on earth. We are ambassadors of Christ and of heaven. Before any nation goes to war, it calls home its ambassadors. Heaven is about to go to war with the earth, so it makes sense for heaven's ambassadors to be called home.

From chapter 4 until the end of chapter 19, God is not once addressed as "Father." He is called God, Lord, Almighty, and other names by which He was known in the Old Testament, but the name "Father," by which He has been known to the church, is entirely absent, with the exception of Revelation 14:1, where He is mentioned as the Father of Christ, but not of the believer.

## The Spirit of God's Transfer From Earth to Heaven

There has been a change in the location of the Holy Spirit. He is said to be in the midst of the churches on earth in chapters 2 and 3, but in Revelation 4:5, the Holy Spirit is in heaven.

## The Symbolic Presence of John in Heaven

In John 21:20-24, the apostle John, the "disciple whom Jesus loved," is told he would tarry until the second coming of Christ. This could only be a true statement in the sense that John was alive in Revelation 1 when God caught him up in the spirit, sent him through thousands of years of time, and set him down in the Tribulation, where he was shown the second coming of Jesus Christ. As we know, John did die, but through his heavenly vision he saw the Lord's coming before he died.

So between chapters 3 and 4, the Rapture of the church has taken place, and now the church is in heaven. The church will not go through the Tribulation, since the Tribulation occurs on the earth and the church is no longer present on the earth.

As we begin our study of Revelation 4, we look through an open door into heaven (v. 1). This chapter answers the question: WHAT IS GOING ON IN HEAVEN WHILE THE TRIBULATION IS GOING ON HERE ON THE EARTH?

## Everyone is Worshiping Around the Throne of God

The word "throne" is one of the key words in Revelation. It occurs some 46 times throughout the book and, in chapter 4 alone, it is found 14 times. It represents one of the great themes of Revelation: the sovereignty of God over all of His universe.

## Seated Upon the Throne is the Triune God (vv. 2-3)

" . . . and One sat on the throne" (v. 2) and " . . . He who sat" (v. 3) are primarily references to God the Father. A description of God is possible only by comparison. Jasper, to which He is compared, is a clear gem like our diamond. Sardius is a red stone comparable to the ruby. The diamond

may refer to God's glory and the ruby to His
sacrifice.

### Surrounding the Throne is a Rainbow (v. 3)

This rainbow was of differing shades of emerald green. It was
a complete circle and not an arc as we see it. In heaven all things
are completed. Usually the rainbow appears after the storm; here
it appears before the storm. The rainbow spoke of God's mercy
and faithfulness.

### Sitting Around the Throne are the 24 Elders (v. 4)

The 24 elders seated upon the 24 thrones do not represent
the angels or the 12 tribes of Israel. These elders represent
the church-age saints, in the same way that the 24 elders of
the Old Testament represented the entire body of priests. In
1 Chronicles 24, we learn that the priesthood numbered in the
thousands. It was impossible for all of the priests to go into the
temple at the same time, so the Levitical priesthood was represented every two weeks by an order of 24 priests. When those
24 priests were in the temple ministering, they were a representative body. The 24 elders in heaven are such a body also.
The context of Revelation, referring to the 24 elders, will shed
light on this. We can know they are representative of the church
age saints by: (1) the praise on their lips (Revelation 5:8-9), (2) the
clothes on their bodies (Revelation 19:7-8), and (3) the crowns
upon their heads (Revelation 4:4). Each of these three elements is
promised to the church (Revelation 3:18; 3:21; 2:10).

### Spread Before the Throne is a Sea of Glass (v. 6)

It is not possible to perfectly identify the meaning of this sea
of glass. However, it is a common description of the area in heaven
which surrounds the throne of God (Exodus 24:10). It is possible
that this is the same material with which the streets of the heavenly
city are paved, as referred to in Revelation 21:21.

Perhaps the interpretation of this sea of glass is as Henry Alford
suggests: "The primary reference will be to the clear ether in which
the throne of God is upborne and the intent of setting this space
in front of the throne will be to betoken its separation and insula-
tion from the place where the Seer stood and indeed from all else
about it." [1]

## Situated in the Midst of the Throne are the Four Living Creatures (vv. 6-8)

Although there is conjecture concerning the identity of these four living creatures, there are three major views as to their identity.

The first view is that they represent the four Gospels. Here it is held that the four living creatures represent the four major aspects of the person of Jesus Christ as seen in the four Gospels. As the Lion of the tribe of Judah, He thus represents the King in the gospel of Matthew. As the calf or ox, He is the Servant of Jehovah, the Faithful One of Mark. As man, He is the human Jesus, presented in the gospel of Luke. As the eagle, He is the divine Son of God presented in the gospel of John. This seems the least likely interpretation.

The second view, as taught by Louis Talbot, holds that "These living creatures are not created beings, because John says they are 'in the midst of the throne.' They are one with it, round about it, and seem to guard the throne of God; but they are also in the midst of it and are part of it. These four living creatures are none other than the attributes of the great God who sits upon the throne." [2] He identifies the four attributes as majesty, strength, personality, and omniscience.

The third view, that the four living creatures represent the angels whose function it is to bring glory to God, would appear to be the proper interpretation based on the evidence found elsewhere in Scripture. It is always best to let the Bible interpret the Bible. In Ezekiel 1:4-14, the four living creatures are described. In Ezekiel 10:14-17 they are identified. Isaiah 6:1-3 describes the seraphim in a very similar way to Ezekiel.

The four living creatures are the cherubim, or angels of God, and they are involved in two ways: they minister to the holiness of God in worship, and they execute His judgments on the world as seen in association with the first four seals (Revelation 6:1, 3, 5, 7). It was also the four living creatures who gave the seven angels the bowls of wrath that are poured out upon the earth as the last judgment of the Tribulation period (Revelation 15:7).

## Singing Praise to the Throne are the Angels and the Church (vv. 9-11)

This is the worship of the glorified Christ, who is the Creator of the world (John 1:1-3, 10). God is just about to deal with the physical earth in judgment, and before He does, the Creator of that earth is worshiped by the church in heaven.

There is a wonderful truth wrapped up in the difference between the worship of the angels and the worship of the elders. As the four living creatures glorify God, the elders fall down before the throne and praise Him. The Book of Revelation is filled with hymns of praise (4:8-11; 5:9-13; 7:12-17; 11:15-18; 12:10-12; 15:3-4; 16:5-7; 19:1-6).

The living creatures (angels) can only celebrate and declare. They worship in the third person as witnesses to the whole process of redemption. The elders (church) worship with understanding and spiritual intelligence. They worship in the second person because they know the joy of salvation. Walter Scott explains why: "The worship of the elders is of a different character to that of the Living Ones. Theirs is the worship of redeemed persons who, as having the mind of Christ, enter intelligently into the thoughts of God and who know Him personally in His holiness and love. It is the worship of persons whose hearts have been won by His exceeding great love and whose consciences have been cleansed by faith in the divine testimony to the precious blood of Christ." [3]

APPLICATION REVELATION 4:1-11

1. In Revelation 4:2-3, there is "One" who occupies the throne in heaven. Read Revelation 5:6 and note who is mentioned and where He is in relation to the throne.

Now read Revelation 4:5 and note the same things.

In Revelation 3:21, who is speaking, and where is He in relation to the throne?

Now list the possibilities as to who occupies the throne in Revelation 4:2-3, and give your reasons.

2. In Revelation 4:1 and 1 Thessalonians 4:16, the word "voice" is mentioned. Describe the voice.

In those same passages, there also appears the word "trumpet." Note what is said about it there in relationship to the "trumpet" spoken of in 1 Corinthians 15:52.

Read Revelation 4:2 and 1 Corinthians 15:52-53 and record any changes you notice.

To what event do you think these passages refer?

3. Revelation 4:1 describes an open door in heaven. In Revelation 3:20, a door is also mentioned. Note who is standing there, what He promises, and what must be done to receive the promise. You may need to review Revelation 1 for the context.

Have you taken those actions? Do you have the assurance in your heart (1 John 3:19-21) that you have taken those actions?

Write a prayer to indicate your response to Revelation 3:20.

4. Revelation 4:3 speaks of a rainbow. A rainbow is also mentioned in Genesis 9:8-17. What did it signify in the Genesis passage?

Who initiated it?

To whom did He give the rainbow?

How long was it intended to be a "sign"?

In what ways can you personally identify with this "sign"?

5. In Revelation 4:4, the 24 elders are wearing golden crowns on their heads. In Revelation 4:10, they cast their crowns before the throne. Read the following Scriptures and note the crowns that are awarded and who receives them.

1 Corinthians 9:25-26a

James 1:12

1 Thessalonians 2:19-20

1 Peter 5:1-4

2 Timothy 4:8

6. What crowns will you receive?


7. Revelation 4 ends with all eyes in heaven on the throne and all voices offering praise to our Lord and our God, the only One worthy to receive praise. Meditate on Revelation 4:8. Write down why He is worthy to receive your praise.


**DID YOU KNOW?**

There are two different Greek words used in Revelation for crowns. One is *diadema*, the crown of a ruler or sovereign, the crown of governmental authority. The other, *stephanos*, is the crown of a victor, which was awarded in the Greek games when a person won a race or athletic contest. The word for crown in Revelation 4:4, 10 is *stephanos*.

---

[1] Henry Alford, *The Greek New Testament* (Chicago: Moody Press, 1958), 598.
[2] Louis T. Talbot, *The Revelation of Jesus Christ* (Grand Rapids: Wm. B. Eerdmans Publishing Co., 1937), 73.
[3] Walter Scott, *Exposition of the Revelation of Jesus Christ* (London: Pickering & Inglis Ltd., nd), 129.

# Deed to the Earth

In this lesson we will begin to study the book,
or scroll, which is the focus of John's attention
as he looks at the throne in heaven.

OUTLINE  R E V E L A T I O N  5 : 1 - 1 4

The scene opens on the throne of God, surrounded by an emerald rainbow and 24 elders representing the church. A sea of glass separates all other creatures, save the angels, from the glory of God and the four living creatures who are God's special angelic servants. As all are praising God, we notice a scroll, or book, taking on significance in this chapter.

I. **The Scroll: Title-deed to the Earth** • Revelation 5:1
A. What it contains
B. What it represents
II. **Who Is Worthy to Unseal the Scroll?** • Revelation 5:2-4
III. **The Worship Begins** • Revelation 5:5-14
A. Identity of the One worshiped
1. The Lion of the tribe of Judah
2. The Root of David
3. The Lamb who was slain
B. Locality of One worshiped
C. Activity of One worshiped
IV. **Aspects of the Worship in Heaven** • Revelation 5:8-14
A. The redeemed worship
B. The angels worship
C. All creation worships
D. The four living creatures and 24 elders worship

Chapters 4 and 5 of Revelation should not be divided. The first word of chapter 5 is "and," which indicates a continuation of the flow of thought from chapter 4. The picture we must remember from chapter 4 is God, seated on His throne and surrounded by angelic beings and elders representing the church of Jesus Christ. Thunder, lightning, and voices are heard, signifying the judgment which is about to fall on the earth.

The focus of John's attention is on the scroll in the right hand of the One who sits on the throne. The scroll was rolled up like a wheel and had on it seven seals. In the same way, Roman law required that a will be rolled up and sealed seven times. The fact that this scroll was written on both the front and the back is an indication that it was full and nothing more could be added.

## What the Book or Scroll Contains

Revelation 5:9 speaks of a book with seals to be opened. As we look at chapter 6, the seals begin to be opened, and we see the judgments of God poured out upon the earth. These indicate the beginning of the Tribulation period on the earth. The number seven is mentioned three times during the Tribulation period, referring first to seals, then to trumpets, and then to bowls. These are related to each other as in a telescope, with the seven trumpets being contained within the seventh seal and the seven bowls being contained within the seventh trumpet. The seals, then, are all the judgments for the entire Book of Revelation, from beginning to end of the Tribulation period. As the scroll is unrolled the seals are broken one by one, slowly revealing what is going to happen.

## What the Book or Scroll Represents

There has been a great deal of discussion among students of the Word of God as to what the scroll might signify. Some hold that the scroll is the book of the new covenant. Others feel that this is the revelation of God's purpose and counsel concerning the world. A third opinion holds, I feel, the correct identification of the scroll or book: the title-deed to the earth. It rests in the hand of God as He is seated on the throne in glory, and it unfolds the rest of the Book of Revelation in its entirety.

## Who is Worthy to Open the Scroll or Book? (vv. 2-4)

John, the receiver of the revelation, openly weeps as he hears the angel proclaim with a loud voice, "Who is worthy to open the scroll, and to loose its seals?" He discovers there is One who is found worthy, as he is told, "Do not weep. Behold . . ." (v. 5). This begins the worship of Revelation 5:5-14.

## Identity of the One Worshiped (v. 5)

Three names are given in the text to identify the One who takes the scroll.

The first name given is the "Lion of the tribe of Judah." In Genesis 49:8-12, Jacob prophesied to Judah that out of the tribe of Judah would come the Messiah, who is Jesus Christ. One of the names for the Messiah is the Lion of the tribe of Judah. King David was from the tribe of Judah, and one of the common titles for Jesus while He was on earth was the "Son of David." This title speaks of dignity, sovereignty, courage, and victory.

The second name given in the text is "Root of David." This is one of the most interesting names for Jesus Christ in the text. As far as Jesus' humanity was concerned, He had His roots in David. He came from the tribe of Judah through the descent of David, who was from the tribe of Judah. But notice, the text doesn't say the root was *in* David; rather, the root was *of* David. That places Jesus before David in ancestry. Jesus was both the ancestor of David and his root. In His humanity, Jesus was from David and in His deity He was before David. What a wonderful term for Jesus Christ as He is about to take the scroll and unfold the eternal plan of God, for He is the eternal God Himself!

The third name is the greatest of all three! Jesus is now presented as the Lamb who was slain. The word "lamb," referring to Jesus Christ, is used in this book 28 times. In Genesis 22, Isaac asked his father, Abraham, "Where is the lamb . . . ?" In John 1, we are told, "Behold, the Lamb of God . . ." Now John sees that this One who is about to take the title-deed to the earth is the Lamb.

## Four Facts About the Lamb (vv. 6-7)

First, the Lamb is standing in the midst of the throne. This is not the position you would expect a slain lamb to be in. A slain lamb lies down, but this one is standing. This is a picture of the resurrected Christ in heaven, standing in the midst of the throne. In heaven, the Lord is usually pictured as being seated, signifying that the work of redemption is completed. But now the slain Lamb is standing, ready to move out from the glory of heaven to the earth where judgment is going to break out. There He will reclaim the earth.

Secondly, the slain Lamb is standing, suggesting that the marks of the death of Jesus Christ will be visible throughout eternity. When we see Jesus in heaven we will see the same thing the disciples and apostles saw after He came out of the grave. We will never be allowed to forget that it was through His death that we have made entrance into heaven, where we will spend eternity, or that we are there because Jesus loved us enough to die on the cross for our sins.

The third important thing to note about this Lamb is that He is strong. The picture of seven horns is a picture of strength. Even though the Lamb was slain, He has not been weakened. He has the strength necessary to fulfill His promises to the redeemed of this earth.

The fourth noteworthy fact is that He is searching. The seven eyes represent His all-seeing wisdom. The seven eyes are said to be the seven spirits sent out into all the earth. He is the omniscient and omnipresent God!

Many comparisons can be made between the Lion and the Lamb. The Lamb is a reference to His first coming, when He died on the cross. The Lion is a reference to His second coming, when He will judge. The Lamb is symbolic of His meekness, the Lion of His majesty. As the Lamb, He is the Savior; as the Lion, He is sovereign. As the Lamb, He is judged; as the Lion, He is judging. The Lamb represents the grace of God; the Lion represents the government of God.

## Locality of the One Worshiped (v. 6)

The Lamb described above is found in the midst of the throne of God. We worship Him because of where He is.

## Activity of the One Worshiped (vv. 6-7)

First, He takes the book out of the right hand of Him who sits upon the throne. Here Jesus reclaims His authority over all the earth. He receives the kingdom from His Father and takes control of it through the Tribulation period in preparation for the Millennium, when He will reign forever and ever.

The second thing that happens is that He receives the worship of heaven. When the Lamb takes the scroll, the weeping ends and the praising begins. Notice that until Jesus came forth, John was weeping; but as soon as Jesus comes and takes the book, praise brakes out in heaven.

The central focus of this chapter is on worship; it is a treatise on worship. No one is really capable of unfolding all the truths about worship in these closing verses.

## Aspects of Worship in Heaven (vv. 8-14)

It is possible that the "prayers of the saints" referred to in Revelation 5:8 is the prayer that Jesus taught His disciples in Matthew 6:9-13. The phrase "Your kingdom come. Your will be done on earth as it is in heaven" is ultimately going to be fulfilled when the Lord takes control of this earth. Not until that time will this prayer be fully answered.

Every aspect of sacred music seems to be reflected in the hymn that is recorded in Revelation 5:9-10. Warren Wiersbe has called it "a worship hymn, a missionary hymn, a gospel song, a devotional hymn, and a prophetic hymn."[1]

And then there are the choruses in this antiphonal song. In verses 8-10, the redeemed, or believers, worship. Then in verses 11-12, there are new participants. Literally, the angels are innumerable as they begin to proclaim the worthiness of the Lamb who has received the scroll.

In verse 13, the chorus of praise is joined by every creature in heaven, on the earth, under the earth, and in the sea—all saying, "Blessing and honor and glory and power be to Him who sits on the throne, and to the Lamb . . ." Praise goes out from the throne like ripples of water because of the redemption wrought by the Lamb who was slain.

Finally, in verse 14, the four living creatures proclaim "Amen!" and the twenty-four elders who represent the church fall down and worship the Lamb.

If you are a believer, you can sing praise directly to God because of the joy of your redemption and the triumph you have in Christ. The angels can only sing "about" it because they have never experienced personally the joy that salvation brings.

It is possible that the thing that will fuel the fire of praise in heaven forever and ever is the knowledge that we are the redeemed children of God. The crescendo of praise will grow and grow as the years go by for eternity. The longer we are in heaven, the more we will know about how much we have to be happy.

The song we will sing forever and ever is "Worthy is the Lamb that was slain."

---

**APPLICATION REVELATION 5 : 1 - 1 4**

1. Does God have control over the world today? Read the following Scriptures and note what you learn about who rules the world.

Ephesians 2:2

John 12:31

John 14:30

Why does Jesus say, "he has nothing in Me"?

John 16:11

2. In 2 Corinthians 4:4, the apostle Paul identifies the one who blinds the minds of unbelievers. What is his title?

3. Is God sovereign over this world and the "prince"? Read Daniel 4:35 and record your answer.

4. What does Job 42:2 have to say about God's sovereignty?

5. Read Paul's prayer for the believers in Ephesus, found in Ephesians 1:18-23. Record who has power and over what He has power.

6. In Colossians 1:12-18, the Father (God) has qualified us to share in the inheritance of the saints in light, delivered us from the power of darkness, translated us into the kingdom of the Son of His love. What do we have in the Son?

How is the Son described?

7. In summary, what have you learned about the control of the earth—past, present, and future?

8. God revealed much of the future to the prophet Daniel. What did God tell him concerning that prophecy in Daniel 12:8-9?

9. What relationship do you see between the Daniel passage and what John is about to see unsealed in Revelation 5?

10. Read Matthew 22:41-46. Note the question Jesus asked the Pharisees.

11. Jesus is called the "Root of David" in Revelation 5:5. This reflects both His humanity and His deity. Read Philippians 2:5-11 and record what you learn about the humanity and deity of Christ.

12. Read the account of the disciple Thomas, found in John 20:24-28, and note what you learn about the marks that will be visible for eternity on the Lamb of Revelation 5:6.




What was Thomas' response upon seeing and touching the marks?


Have you doubted your Lord? What have you "seen" of the risen Lord that has made you believe?




13. Jesus said that the Father would send you a Helper, the Spirit of truth (John 14:16-17), that this Helper would teach you all things (John 14:26), and that He would guide you into all truth (John 16:13). Romans 8:1-4 reminds us that we are to "walk according to the Spirit." Why?




Now read Romans 8:5-9 and note what you learn about the contrasts between flesh and Spirit in these verses.




14. Do you walk according to the flesh or according to the Spirit?

15. Read what 1 John 1:9 says we can do to deal with our sins. Write it out. Do you believe that?

16. Read Isaiah 61:3 and list the exchanges that are made when we have been set free from our captivity to sin.

What will we be called when we have made these exchanges?

What will be the result?

17. Write out your own "hymn of praise" to God, based on your study today. It will bring glory to God.

DID YOU KNOW?

No place in the Bible, with the possible exception of a reference in the Book of Job, are we ever told that angels can sing. The Scriptures record that angels "say," not "sing," their praises to God.

---

[1] Warren Wiersbe, *Be Victorious* (Wheaton, IL: Victor Books, 1985)

# The Four Horsemen of the Apocalypse

In this lesson the first four of the seven seals
are broken to reveal the events that will usher
in the seven years of trouble on earth.

OUTLINE    R E V E L A T I O N    6 : 1 - 8

Worship is the theme of chapters 4 and 5, but wrath is the subject of chapter 6. Each of the seven seals is broken as the
scroll is unrolled and all of the Tribulation period is outlined for
us. We will study these seals that are on the title-deed to the
earth, focusing in this lesson on the first four seals.

  I. **Two Introductory Thoughts**
     A. Interpretation of the phrase "come and see"
     B. Significance of the horse
 II. **The Four Seals in Revelation 6:1-8**
     A. First, the white horse • Antichrist
     B. Second, the red horse • War
     C. Third, the black horse • Famine
     D. Fourth, the pale horse • Death and Hell
III. **Responses to the Future Trouble**
     A. Praise
     B. Passion
     C. Personal evaluation

The subject of chapters 6-19 is the beginning of the day of God's wrath. Man's day on earth is dying and Jesus, the Worthy Lamb of chapter 5, is about to take back control of the earth. The four broken seals in this section reveal the events that will bring in the seven years of tribulation. The action of the Book of Revelation begins in chapter 6 as John, the receiver of the revelation, hears someone saying, "Come and see." We will discover what those words mean and to whom they were spoken.

### The Interpretation of the Phrase "Come and See"

The Greek word *erkou*, translated "come" may also be translated "go" or "proceed." Look at it in its context and observe what happens when the command is given each time. In each instance, when one of the angels cries *"erkou,"* a rider and horse proceed across the stage of history, summoned to go forth upon the earth.

### The Significance of the Horse

It is difficult for us today to understand the significance of the imagery of the horse used here. The Jews held the horse in great awe and reverence. To them, horses represented God's activity on earth and the forces He used to accomplish His divine purposes. Job 39:19-25 carries a vivid description of the horse. It is very probable that the imagery of the horses in Revelation 6 is connected to the vision of the Old Testament prophet in Zechariah 6:1-8.

### The First Seal—The White Horse (v. 2)

The white horse in Oriental imagery is the symbol of a conqueror. Here, in the first part of the Tribulation, the white horse rides across the earth. Some are persuaded that this is a reference to Jesus Christ, who is said to be on a white horse in Revelation 19:11. This cannot be the correct interpretation for several reasons.

First, His weapon in Revelation 6 is a bow without any arrows, whereas in Revelation 19 it is a sword. Secondly, in chapter 6 the crown is a *stephanos,* the victor's crown. In chapter 19, Christ wears a *diadema,* the kingly crown, upon His head. And finally, in chapter 6, the first appearance of judgment on the earth is just the beginning. In chapter 19, the white horse signifies the end of the time of judgment. Christ is the climax of tribulation; He ends it all!

The rider upon the white horse is none other than the false Christ or the Antichrist, riding into the world at the beginning of the Tribulation period and bringing peace to the world; hence, his bow has no arrows. He conquers peacefully. The event that begins the Tribulation is the Antichrist's covenant with the people of Israel and their belief in his protection.

### The Second Seal—The Red Horse (vv. 3-4)

The rider on this second horse personifies war. He takes away the peace the Antichrist has established on earth. He will appear to be the answer to every man's needs. Since the day Cain killed his brother, Abel, the world has known very little else but war. Someone has estimated that in 5,560 years of recorded history, there have been more than 14,550 wars. Of the 128 or so conflicts since 1898, more than 73 of them have taken place since World War II.

The rider of the red horse was given a great sword. There is a Greek word *(hromphaiai)* for the sword used by a soldier when he is marching to war. However, here in chapter 6 we find the word *machaira*, which is the assassin's sword, the kind of weapon used to cut the throat of an animal or a man.

Thus, the red horseman represents not only nation rising against nation and kingdom against kingdom, but man fighting against individual man. It is a time of murder, assassination, bloodshed, revolution, and war, which break out in every aspect we can possibly comprehend. There is no major section of the world today where some kind of conflict is not going on or about to start.

### The Third Seal—The Black Horse (vv. 5-6)

War and famine usually go together. The color black is often connected with famine. A shortage of food will always drive up prices and force the government to ration what is available.

The denarius referred to in the text was the standard daily wage for laborers (Matthew 20:2). A quart of wheat was about the very least amount of food that could sustain one person for one day.

The text also says that oil and wine, considered the rich

man's luxuries, were to be exempted from this judgment. In other words, the affluent will escape major hardship and the masses will be hungry.

Already today, more than half of the world goes to bed hungry every night. Malnutrition claims the lives of 10,000 people every day. The garbage of one home in the United States would feed a family of six each day in India. The average American dog has a higher protein diet than most of the peoples of the world.

## The Fourth Seal—The Pale Horse (vv. 7-8)

John now sees two personages—Death is riding a pale horse and Hell (the realm of the dead) follows after him. Note that as these two ride forth, they are armed with weapons: swords, hunger, death, and wild beasts. Ezekiel 14:21 describes these weapons as the "four severe judgments." History shows that, in the past, there has been a very close association between these four.

Historians tell us that an estimated 26 million people died of the epidemics of influenza and typhoid after World War I—more than died in the war itself. Today we are on the verge of the worst plague the world has ever known: one that will kill more people than have died in all of the plagues yet known to man. It is Acquired Immune Deficiency Syndrome (AIDS). William Haseltine, a leading AIDS researcher at the Harvard Medical School in Boston, said in a recent New York Times article entitled "Top Officials and Experts Urge More AIDS Funds": "The AIDS epidemic will produce an enormous and frightening effect on world health that public officials may be relatively powerless to contain."[1]

It is interesting to note from the Ezekiel 14 passage that the pestilence will be in connection with "beasts." The reference here is probably symbolic. It refers to beast-like men. The Greek word for beast appears 38 times in Revelation and on all other occasions it has to do with the Beast, the false messiah. It is also possible to link the "beasts" here with the famine and plague. The most destructive creatures on earth are rats, the greatest menace to human health and food supplies. Rats carry about 35 different diseases.

Whatever your interpretation, the rider on this fourth horse will reap a terrible harvest from the earth. He kills 25% of the entire population of the world.

This prediction by John perfectly aligns with Jesus' prophecy found in Matthew 24:3-7. Then Jesus adds the most frightening statement: "All these are the beginning of sorrows" (Matthew 24:8).

As we contemplate this future time of trouble, what response should we have?

## The Response of Praise

If we have understood clearly the teaching of chapters 4 and 5, we who know the Lord as personal Savior ought to rejoice in His provision for us, though we mourn for those here on the earth who will be suffering. While the Tribulation is mounting in momentum below, we will be worshiping the Lamb around the throne of God.

## The Response of Passion

Although the events of the seven years of tribulation belong entirely to that time, they will not begin suddenly without some warning beforehand. Future events cast their shadows before them. The problems will begin to intensify before the Tribulation. Surely that fact ought to make us look with a sense of urgency on the task which is ours as believers. Prophecy, correctly understood, should be the greatest motivation to evangelism.

## The Response of Personal Evaluation

If you are reading this message as an unbeliever; if you have never personally asked Jesus Christ to be your Savior; if your interest in prophecy is one of curiosity, please understand that the time of opportunity for you is now. The writer of Hebrews asks you a most sobering question: "How shall we escape if we neglect so great a salvation . . . ?" (Hebrews 2:3).

1. The Old Testament prophet Daniel wrote of similar events to Revelation 6. In Daniel 9:26-27, he refers to someone "who is to come." Who is he?

What will he do?

2. Isaiah 14:12-15 reveals this "prince" to us. What title is he given?

What are his desires?

What is his end?

3. Now read Ezekiel 28:12-19. How is the "king of Tyre" described in verses 12-15?

What happened in verse 15 that brought a change?

How did his description change in verses 16-19?

What is his end?

4. In Luke 10:18, how did Jesus describe what happened to this "prince"?

5. The apostle Paul in 2 Corinthians 11:14 reminds us of an important truth about this "prince." What is it?

6. Now how do you see all these Scriptures relating to the rider of the white horse of Revelation 6:2? Who is he?

7. Jesus Himself gave witness to the prophetic events described in Revelation. Read Matthew 24:6, 21, 22 and list what He says.

8. Read Jeremiah 14:1-2 and Lamentations 5:10 and indicate what they have to say about famine.




9. In Matthew 14:13-21 is the account of Jesus' response to the need of the multitude. What was their need and how did He respond to it?




What does verse 14 say was His motivation?




10. Will He provide for you? Why?




Are you afraid you will not have what you need? Read Philippians 4:19 and record God's promise to you.

11. Revelation 6:8 refers to "Death . . . and Hades." Read Revelation 1:18 and record what you find. Is it an encouragement to you? How?

12. Since our response to all this should first be one of praise, write out your praise to God in light of your study this week.

13. Another response we should have is one of urgency regarding the salvation of loved ones, friends, co-workers, etc. Write out what steps of action you plan to take.

14. Remembering that 2 Corinthians 13:5 says we are to make a personal evaluation of ourselves, write out your present relationship with the Lord and what you may need to do to improve it.

15. Why should you care about seals, scrolls, horsemen, etc? What difference should your study this week make in your lifestyle?

DID YOU KNOW:

The scroll was an ancient roll or document upon which traditional wills were printed. The seals were not all on the final edge of the scroll, but were placed throughout the roll so that as each seal was broken more truth was unveiled, a little more each time.

---

[1] "Top Officials and Experts Urge More AIDS Funds," *New York Times*, 27 September 1985.

# The Souls Under the Altar

In this lesson we will look at the fifth seal and the souls under the altar, which picture the suffering and persecution that will take place during the Tribulation period.

OUTLINE    R E V E L A T I O N    6 : 9 - 1 1

The fifth seal does not present the action itself, but rather the result of the action. In the first four seals we saw the judgment develop, but in the fifth seal we are allowed to see only the result. Under the altar, John sees the souls of those who have already been slain, and we are left only to imagine the suffering they must have endured.

I. **The Context of Their Martyrdom**
   A. Who are these martyrs?
   B. How will people be saved during the Tribulation?
   C. What happens after they are saved?
II. **The Cause of Their Martyrdom**
III. **The Consequence of Their Martyrdom**
IV. **The Cry of Their Martyrdom**
V. **The Comfort of Their Martyrdom**
   A. Refuge
   B. Rest
   C. Robe
VI. **Three Applications Concerning God**

The history of redemption has been written in the blood of martyrs, from the Old Testament to the New Testament. Even in modern times we see many examples of martyrdom, among whom are Chinese believers who dared to meet together despite the communist law and Russian believers who defied the authorities by owning a Bible.

What of God's people, the Jews? One modern example is Hitler's persecution and extermination of the Jews in Europe, which was so great that the Jewish population of the world was probably reduced to less than the number of Jews who left Egypt under Moses.

The living creatures in the first four seals (Revelation 6:1-8) are connected with the unseen powers behind the human agents of persecution upon the earth. The last three seals present an even more ominous picture as God begins to intervene personally in the affairs of men on the earth. This pattern of four and three will also be found in the trumpet judgments and the bowl judgments. In each case, the last three judgments are more severe than the previous four.

John also tells us that the end of it all has not yet come. There will be still more martyrs in the future. The souls under the altar provide a picture of the untold suffering and persecution that will take place during the Tribulation. We will examine their martyrdom in several ways.

## The Context of Their Martyrdom

Who are these martyrs? First of all, we need to remember that the church of Jesus Christ has already been raptured and the dead in Christ have been resurrected. So, these martyrs are not from the church age.

Secondly, since the martyrs ask for judgment upon those who dwell on the earth, it is obvious that their murderers are still living. This would strongly suggest that these martyrs have come from the Tribulation scene on the earth and are the faithful saints martyred in the early part of the Tribulation period. No doubt they are casualties of the first four seal judgments. When the church is taken away God is going to deal with Israel once more, and Israel as a nation will be saved. Many Jews will turn to God and reject the Antichrist during the Tribulation. Because of this, the Antichrist will make their blood run like a river; many will be martyred.

How will people be saved during the Tribulation if there are no believers on earth at the beginning of the seven years of tribulation?

For one thing, God will have sent His two witnesses into the world to prophesy and perform mighty miracles. Somehow, there will be 144,000 Israelites "sealed" for God's service during this period (Revelation 7:4).

It is possible that another means will also be used. Dr. Henry Morris has suggested a "silent witness": ". . . millions upon millions of copies of the Bible and Bible portions . . . will not be removed and multitudes will no doubt be constrained to read the Bible in those days . . . and will turn to their Creator and Savior . . . and will be willing to give their testimony for the Word of God and even to give their lives as they seek to persuade the world that the calamities it is suffering are judgments from the Lord." [1]

What will happen after they are saved? Martyrdom will be as common then as it is uncommon today. Those who trust in God at that time will be called upon to demonstrate their faith—often with their lives.

## The Cause of Their Martyrdom

The martyrs of Revelation 6 were slain for the same reason John was exiled: "I, John, both your brother and companion in tribulation . . . was on the island that is called Patmos for the word of God and for the testimony of Jesus Christ" (Revelation 1:9).

The "word of their testimony" is very likely a reference to the words of judgment they will preach. As the events of the Tribulation begin to intensify, these blood-bought believers will begin to warn others of even more severe judgment to come. They will preach repentance and judgment and they will be killed for their message. These saints have been sacrificed upon the altar of their devotion to God.

Revelation 19:19-21 warns that all who receive the mark of the Beast, which we know is the number 666, will suffer eternal judgment at the hand of God. The converse is also true: Those who refuse to receive this mark will suffer the wrath of the Antichrist instead.

Remember that with the Rapture of the church the restraint of the Holy Spirit will be removed. The world rulers of that day will view followers of Christ as objects upon which they can vent their anger and rebellion against God.

Dr. W. A. Criswell reminds us of the true character of the prophet of God: ". . . whenever there is a true prophet of God, he will preach judgment . . . (today) we stand up and speak of the love of Jesus, and we speak of peace, and we speak of all things pretty and beautiful. But remember, these other things are as real. The same book that tells us about good, tells us about bad . . . . The Bible that presents the Lord Jesus as the Savior is the same Bible that presents to us the Devil as our enemy and adversary of damnation and destruction. The two go together." [2]

In that day, the Jews who have given their lives to Christ will once again know the pain of suffering and slaughter.

## The Consequence of Their Martyrdom

As the fifth seal is opened the scene shifts from earth back to heaven, and John sees a vision of those who are going to be martyred for their faith. They are described as being under the altar, in keeping with the fact that the blood of the Old Testament sacrifice was poured out under the altar (Exodus 29:12; Leviticus 4:7). The pouring of the blood was the sign that the sacrifice had been completed and the effect of the sacrifice was in place. As John watches, he hears them cry out with a loud voice asking why God has not judged those who took their lives.

The fact that they are under the altar is an indication of their justification. They are protected by the blood of Jesus Christ and are "covered," or justified in God's sight.

## The Cry of Their Martyrdom

The imprecatory cry of these martyrs in Revelation 6:10 is more evidence that they are not church age sufferers. The cry of the church age martyr is the cry of Stephen, the first martyr of the church, "Lord, do not charge them with this sin"(Acts 7:60). If they were living in the church age, their cry for vengeance would be improper. The persecuted Jew of the Tribulation will be able to call for God's judgment in perfect propriety. The age of grace has been closed. This is the day of the judgment of God.

When these martyrs address the Lord, they use a name for

Him that is not found in any other passage in Revelation. The word translated as the word "Lord" is the Greek word *despotes*, from which we get our word "despot." It implies supreme authority, absolute power, and sovereign control and shows God's absolute control over all the affairs of men and of the world.

## The Comfort of Their Martyrdom

Revelation 6:11 is the Lord's answer to their cry—the cup of iniquity is not yet full. But in verses 9 and 11 we see a picture of the compassionate heart of a loving God. There are three things that speak of comfort for these martyrs.

The first is that they are given a refuge, in verse 9, under the altar. This speaks of protection. Nobody can get through the blood of Christ to harm them anymore.

Second, they are given a rest in verse 11. When these martyrs ask how long it will be until they are avenged for their deaths, they are told that it will take a short period of time for the fulfillment of God's program and that still other martyrs will be added to their number before final restitution.

Last, they are given a robe. God, in His gracious love and mercy, rewards each individual martyr with a robe. This gift from the Lord causes us to ask a very interesting question: What kind of bodies do these martyrs have? If these are saints who died during the Tribulation, it is clear from Scripture that they will not receive their own resurrection bodies until the end of the Tribulation. Revelation 20:4-5 indicates that there will be a special resurrection for all Tribulation saints at the very end.

Scholars have been divided as to whether saints who die receive temporary bodies in heaven prior to the resurrection body, or whether only their spiritual beings are in heaven before the resurrection. One such scholar suggests that the fact that they have robes indicates that they must have bodies of some kind. However, it isn't an earthly body or the resurrection body that Christ spoke of having after His resurrection. Perhaps their are temporary bodies to be replaced by resurrection bodies, which will last for eternity, given when Christ returns.

## Three Applications Concerning God

First, God has a plan that includes each detail. Revelation 6:9-11 strikes a deathblow to the idea of "soul sleep." These souls are conscious and speaking. We should not be led astray by the use of the word "sleep" in connection with the death of the body. This is not "soul sleep." We can understand more clearly when we read 2 Thessalonians 4:14-16. Here we are told two things about the resurrection of believers: (1) They rise from the grave, and (2) God will bring them with Christ when He returns. There is only one way to explain how they can both rise and be brought from heaven. The soul and the body are separated in death. "Sleep" is applied only to the believer's body, which goes into the grave and awaits resurrection. "Sleep" is NEVER applied to the soul of the believer.

Then we see that God has a purpose that explains each delay. The Lord would not answer the martyrs' prayer for vengeance yet. The cup of man's iniquity was not yet full. The time before the retribution was measured as a "little while." There were still some "fellow servants" and "brethren" who had to suffer martyrdom before God could act. Surely this proves that God ordains the details. Nothing can touch the believer unless it passes through the will of God. There is a definite plan for the life of every one of God's children. He has cast a hedge around us for protection (Job 1:10).

Last, we see that God has a program that extends to each dispensation. In the hour of God's great judgment upon this earth and upon those who have rejected Him, He still holds out the plan of salvation for those who will believe. Even in this dark hour there are still those who will embrace Him. Now and then, in this dispensation, there are those Jews who acknowledge their Messiah. It will be the same in that day, multiplied many times over.

---

**APPLICATION      REVELATION      6 : 9 - 1 1**

---

1. Deuteronomy 28:64-67 contains a prediction of Moses concerning the Jews. List the details and note any similarities you are aware of in history.

2. In Romans 11:25-26, the apostle Paul makes a prediction concerning the nation of Israel. Write out that prediction. Has it been fulfilled yet?

Do you see any relationship between Paul's prediction and what you have studied in this lesson?

3. Read what the prophet Zechariah said regarding the time of tribulation in Zechariah 13:8-9. What is the "one third" he speaks of?

What does the Lord say He will do with the "one third"?

What do you think it means to be refined "as silver is refined" and tested "as gold is tested"?

4. How does Matthew 24:8-10 compare with the Zechariah passage you just read?

5. Have you ever experienced anything like "refining" or "testing" in your own life?

If so, what result did it produce in you?

What do you think was God's purpose for taking you through that experience?

6. Read Psalm 106:1 and 2 Chronicles 5:13 and record what they say about God.

7. Read 1 John 1:5 and James 1:17. What do they say about God and His activities?

8. Now, what is God's purpose for taking you through any "refining" or "testing" experience?

9. To better understand what happens when we die, read 2 Corinthians 5:8 and Philippians 1:23 and record what the apostle Paul says.

How do these passages help you understand death?

10. Read Job 1:9-12. Who is involved and what are they saying?

Now read Job 2:1-7 and record what you learn from that conversation.

11. Summarize from these two Job passages what you learn about the "hedge" of protection.

12. Read Hebrews 12:5-8, 11 and summarize what you learn about the chastening of God.

13. Romans 8:28, 31-39 indicate how a loving God works in the lives of His people. Write out what you learn from these passages about your relationship to God.

Now write out all the things that you might have considered as separating you from His love. Do they?

14. How much does God love you?

15. How much do you love God? How would He know?

DID YOU KNOW?

The word used to describe the death of these martyrs ("slain") is peculiar in its verb form and might better be translated "slaughtered." It means to slaughter, butcher, or murder, and in all of its uses, with the exception of Revelation 13:3, refers to the killing of Christ or His followers. It is used here in keeping with the special character of these Jewish witnesses whose souls are now beneath the altar of sacrifice in heaven.

[1] Henry Morris, *The Revelation Record* (Wheaton, Illinois: Tyndale House Publishers, Inc., 1983), 119.
[2] W. A. Criswell, *Expository Sermons on Revelation* (Grand Rapids: Zondervan, 1962), 106-107.

# When the Whole World Trembles

The sixth seal is removed in this lesson and it reveals enormous convulsions of nature which devastate the earth and bring terror everywhere.

It would be hard to paint a scene more frightening than this one: a cataclysmic earthquake, the sun becoming black, the moon becoming as blood, the stars falling out of the sky, the heavens being rolled back as a scroll, and the mountains and islands of the sea being moved. It is probable that with the opening of the sixth seal, the first half of the Tribulation is brought to an end.

I. **Three Indicators for This Timing**
   A. The cry of the people (Revelation 6:17)
   B. The coming judgments are more severe than the seal judgments (Revelation 7:1)
   C. The silence of one-half hour (Revelation 8:1)
II. **Five Elements of Judgment in the Sixth Seal** • Revelation 6:12-14
   A. The shaking of the earth
   B. The darkening of the sky
   C. The falling of the stars
   D. The rolling back of the heavens
   E. The moving of the mountains and the islands
III. **The Cry of the Wicked** • Revelation 6:15-17
   A. The responses of sinful men
   B. The hardness of mens' hearts

51

We have, to this point, opened five of the seven seals on the scroll of God, which is the title-deed to the earth. The first seal introduced us to the world's final dictator, Satan's Antichrist. The second revealed a rider on a red horse and brought us face to face with war and bloodshed. The third was a black horse which pictured famine and death. The fourth uncovered the pale horse and revealed the plague of death which will fill the earth. The fifth presented the mass murder of the saints of God in martyrdom. These judgments are largely the result of evil in the hearts of men. The judgment described in the sixth seal is divine punishment inflicted on a sinful world.

The events symbolized by these first six seals take place in the first three and one-half years of the seven years of the Tribulation. We will examine some of the reasons for believing that this sixth seal brings the first half of the Tribulation period to an end.

## Three Indicators for This Timing

Revelation 6:17 refers to people crying as a result of this sixth seal being broken. Their cry is, "For the great day of His wrath has come."

Revelation 7:1 speaks of the four winds of the earth being restrained until 144,000 people can be sealed for protection. These winds represent the blown trumpets and the bowls. The interpretation is clearly that these next judgments are more severe. The seventh seal includes the seven trumpets, and the seventh trumpet includes the seven bowls, indicating a progression in severity.

Finally, the opening of the seventh seal, from which the blown trumpets emerge, is followed by the silence of one-half hour in Revelation 8:1, suggesting an awesome, foreboding sense of fear in view of what is to happen.

When we put these things together with Matthew 24:15-21, which teaches that a marked increase of suffering comes right after the setting up of "the abomination of desolation" spoken of by the prophet Daniel, we can see that this occurs at the midpoint of the Tribulation (Daniel 9:27). It is at this particular time that Israel begins to experience a marked change in the attitude of the Antichrist. Almost overnight, he shifts from being a friend to being a bitter enemy.

These events seem too severe to be taking place this early in the Tribulation. We are only at the end of the first half of the seven years. Some, therefore, have difficulty interpreting Revelation 6:12-17 literally. In order to avoid a literal interpretation, the passage is translated symbolically. The upheaval in the heavens is interpreted as changes in human government, and the changes on earth refer to the upsetting of tradition.

There is, however, one piece of evidence that demands a literal interpretation. Changes in human government could not have created the response of fear that is described in Revelation 6:15. We will look at the characteristics which have created that fear.

## Five Elements of Judgment in the Sixth Seal

Revelation 6:12 says, "Behold, there was a great earthquake..." The Greek word for "quaking" is *seismos*, from which we get our words seismograph and seismology. Jesus prophesied three times that the earthquake described here by John would precede the Day of the Lord. Throughout the Old Testament, the prophets consistently connected the shaking of the earth with this final judgment of the Lord. In fact, the Bible often associates the shaking of the earth with the judgment of the Lord (see Exodus 19:18, Matthew 27:51 and Matthew 28:2). But the earthquake described in Revelation 6:12 will cause widespread destruction and death.

Revelation 6:12 also says, ". . . the sun became black as sackcloth of hair, and the moon became like blood . . .." When Jesus died on the cross, the whole earth became dark at midday. When Egypt was judged, there was a blackness of night. When the Lord came down at Mt. Sinai, the mountain was shrouded in black clouds. The prophets, as well, said a darkness would occur at the beginning of the Tribulation period.

On May 19, 1780, such a dark day occurred in the northeastern part of the United States. The darkness was not caused by cloudiness nor an eclipse of the sun. The cause, even to this day, has never been explained.

When such darkness occurs as the judgment of God, business and pleasure will cease, crime will multiply, and depression of the spirit will settle over the earth. The moon, which reflects the sun's light, will turn to a ghastly red and will frighten even the boldest observer.

In Revelation 6:13, it is recorded that "the stars of heaven fell to the earth . . .." The word "star" here is the Greek word *aster* and it refers to luminous bodies in the sky other than sun and moon. Clearly these "stars" are not the distant stellar objects we know as stars. One writer has identified them as follows: ". . . the language of the text seems to denote more than the meteorites commonly today called falling stars . . . The most likely identification of these particular falling stars is that of a great swarm of asteroids that pummel the earth . . . Scientists have long speculated about the probability of either past or future earth catastrophes caused by encountering a swarm of asteroids . . . " [1]

On the night of November 13, 1833, there was such a shower caused by the passage of the earth across the orbit of a body of meteorites. As the meteorites encountered the earth's atmosphere, they became incandescent and illumined the sky with successive flashes of light. Many people thought that the prophecy of Revelation 6 had come to fulfillment.

In Revelation 6:14, we read the prophecy, ". . . the sky receded as a scroll when it is rolled up." There are two possible explanations for this scientific phenomenon. One is that clouds of dust will gradually spread across the sky, making it appear that the sky is being rolled up. The other is that the earth's crust will be so disturbed by the impact of the asteroids that great segments of it will actually begin to slip and slide over the earth's mantle. Those living in the regions above such shifting will observe the heavens appearing to move in the opposite direction, as if they are being "rolled up." [2]

Finally, Revelation 6:14 says "and every mountain and island was moved out of its place." As John wrote of these events from the island of Patmos, it must have indeed been a strange sensation. This shaking of the earth, darkening of the sky, falling of the stars, rolling back of the heavens, and moving of the mountains and islands will produce a tremendous response in the hearts of all earth-dwellers.

## The Cry of the Wicked

Revelation 6:15-17 reports that a cry will go up from kings, captains, great ones, rich, strong, slave and free. The whole fabric of human society will be terrified. As we examine the responses of sinful men to this great judgment, three timeless truths emerge from the text.

The first truth is sin's horror. No one escapes. No one is exempt. God will work His vengeance upon all sin, for "the great day of His wrath has come, and who is able to stand?" (v. 17)

The second truth is sin's hiding. When the Day of the Lord comes, John sees people seeking somewhere to hide. The terrible thing about sin is that it makes a man a fugitive from God. The supreme thing about the work of Jesus Christ is that it puts man into relationship with God and he no longer seeks to hide.

The third truth is sin's hardness. Instead of calling upon God, these evil men try to hide from the wrath of the Lamb by seeking escape in death. But death only changes their state of existence. Judgment still awaits those who have rejected Christ. They begin to cry out or pray.

One of the most amazing truths of the Book of Revelation is the hardness of men's hearts. Judgment seems to harden them instead of softening them. As the judgments become more severe and the intensity of God's wrath is multiplied throughout the book, the rebellion and stubbornness of sinful men increases. The terrible suffering described in the fifth and sixth trumpet judgments of Revelation 9 should strike terror in the hearts of those remaining. The pouring out of the seven bowls of wrath upon the earth in Revelation 16 should cause them to turn to God and repent of their sin. However, Revelation 19 describes the coming of Christ and His armies to this earth. He will not have any difficulty getting the evil men of the earth to the battlefield. They are so filled with hatred and rebellion that they gladly come to fight. They all gather under the Antichrist in rebellion against God and go off to fight, only to be annihilated.

The wages of sin is death (Romans 6:23). It not only kills the sinner, but it seeks, through that sinner, to kill everyone in its path. There is something insidious about sin. It hardens the heart and callouses the soul and makes men insensitive to the judgment of God. This hardness turns into more sin—sin added to sin until you cannot recover.

There is a message to all of us here. Don't become insensitive to sin, but ask God to make you "naively good." Pray that you won't let the threshold of sin in your life be brought down by the culture in which you live. Pray that you will be sensitive to the slightest inroad of the adversary into your life because sin, when it is finished, brings forth death (James 1:15).

1. 2 Thessalonians 1:6 reminds us of a truth about God's judgment. What is it?

2. Read Psalm 19:9 and record what you learn there about the judgment of God.

3. Read Hebrews 10:26-31. What do these verses reveal about judgment?

Who will receive this judgment?

Why will men be judged?

4. What do the following Scripture passages reveal about earthquakes?

Matthew 24:7

Mark 13:8

Luke 21:11

Do these passages have anything in common with Revelation 6:12?


5. Read the following passages and record what they say about the shaking of the earth.

Ezekiel 38:19


Joel 2:10


Amos 8:8


Haggai 2:6


What event do you think these passages are associated with?


6. Compare Revelation 6:12 with the following passages:

Joel 2:30-31


Zephaniah 1:15


Isaiah 13:9-10

Ezekiel 32:7


Mark 13:24


What event in Revelation are these prophets revealing?


7. Isaiah 34:4 and Revelation 6:14 speak of the same phenomenon. What is it?


8. Jeremiah 4:24 and Nahum 1:5 speak of an event similar to that in Revelation 6:14. What is it?


9. The wicked men in Revelation 6:15-17 seek to hide from their sin. Read Genesis 3:1-10. What did Adam do and why?


Have you ever tried to hide from God when you have sinned?

If so, what was your attitude toward that sin?


Read Genesis 3:11-13 and record Adam and Eve's attitude toward their sin.

10. Read Romans 6:3-9 and record what you learn about Christ and your relationship to Him.

11. Now read Romans 6:11-14 and list the things you are not to do and the things you are to do.

According to Romans 6:14, are these things to be true of you?

12. Read I John 4:15-18. How is our love made perfect?

What does this perfected love produce?

Why?

13. In 2 Corinthians 5:9-10, Paul says our ambition is to be pleasing is to God. Why?

Who is he talking about? You may want to read 2 Corinthians 1:1 to determine to whom he was writing. Also notice the immediate context of 2 Corinthians 5:1-8 for clues.

14. What does 2 Corinthians 5:15 say to you?

For whom are you living? List your reasons for your answer.

15. Write out a prayer of response to the ending message of this lesson overview.

DID YOU KNOW?

The most powerful and widely felt earthquake in American history actually involved three earthquakes. They hit from December 16, 1811 to February 7, 1812, with magnitudes estimated at 8.6, 8.4, and 8.7 on the Richter scale, stronger than either the San Francisco earthquake of 1906 or the Alaskan "Good Friday" earthquake in 1964. They were felt from Canada to Mexico.

---

[1] Henry Morris, *The Revelation Record* (Wheaton, Illinois: Tyndale House Publishers, Inc., 1983), 123.

[2] Ibid.

# Revival in the Tribulation

In this lesson we will see God's people, the Jews, preserved during the judgment of the great Tribulation.

| OUTLINE | REVELATION 7 : 1 - 8 |
|---|---|

Between the sixth and seventh seals, there is an interlude in Revelation 7. It does not advance the narrative of the book, but it is very important to the understanding of this hour of God's judgment. The first six seals of the title-deed to the earth have been removed. Now God is about to seal 144,000 people in a great revival.

   I. **Setting of the Great Revival** • Revelation 7:1
   A. Scene on earth
   B. Scene in heaven
   II. **Sealed Servants of the Great Revival**
   III. **Controversy Presented by this Passage**
   A. What is the seal?
   B. Who are those who are sealed?
   C. Why are they sealed?
   IV. **Identity of the Tribes**
   V. **Most Important Thought from This Passage**

There has never been such a persecuted people as the Jews. And today, even among some Christians, there is a system of thought that divorces the Jewish nation from any further part in the plans and purposes of God. Careful study will illustrate the impossibility of removing God's elective purposes for Israel from the Scriptures. It simply cannot be done without destroying a vast portion of God's Word. John records two visions in this chapter which reveal God at work in His people, Israel.

## Setting of the Great Revival (v. 1)

The picture in Revelation 7 is sketched against the dark background of dread and gloom which the sixth seal reveals. In reality, we must locate this chapter between the "beginning of sorrows" (Matthew 24:8) and the "Great Tribulation" (Matthew 24:21).

There are two separate visions in the text, marked by the Greek phrase *meta tauta eidon*, translated "after these things, I saw." The first vision is recorded in Revelation 7:1-8 and is the scene on earth. The second vision, in Revelation 7:9-17, is a scene in heaven.

The first vision reveals 144,000 representatives of the godly remnant of Israel; it is Jewish in focus and relates the sealing of the servants on earth.

The second vision tells of a great multitude from every nation, kindred, people, and tongue who have been martyred for their faith in Jesus Christ. It is Gentile in focus and reveals the glory of the saints in heaven.

As John is given the first vision, he sees four angels standing at the four corners of the earth. This is not a square earth, but rather the image reflects the four quadrants of the compass, or the four directions. In much the same way our weathermen might report the winds out of the east, so John reports the winds being restrained in all four directions (Revelation 7:1).

The "winds" in Scripture are often the providential agencies employed by God to execute His purposes. Until the elect servants are safe, these winds may not be allowed to blow. Once again, we are impressed by the tremendous power delegated to the angels in God's end-time program.

## Sealed Servants of the Great Revival (vv. 2-8)

The four angels controlling the four winds of the earth are now joined by a fifth angel, who comes from the east and instructs the four angels not to hurt the earth or the sea or the trees until the servants of God are sealed on their foreheads. This reference can be better understood by reading Revelation 8:7-8. The message of the fifth angel is "Do not let the next series of judgments begin until we have sealed the servants of the living God." Some have suggested that this fifth angel is Jesus Christ Himself. The text actually says he "ascends from the east" (Revelation 7:2). In any case, his voice is loud and authoritative, and reaches the four corners of the earth.

## Controversy Presented by the Passage

The first of several questions we must ask of this passage (Revelation 7:2) is, "What is the seal?" The only information given in the text is that it served to protect the servants of God from judgments on the earth. However, this is not the first time God has "sealed" some of His people from judgment and tribulation. Exodus 12:1-27 tells us that God sealed the first-born of all the Jewish families who were faithful in applying the blood to the doorposts as they were instructed.

There is also the seal of the Antichrist, mentioned in Revelation 13. That seal, the number 666, will be branded on the forehead or hand of those who have sworn allegiance to this false Christ. According to the revelation, without that seal it will be impossible to purchase food or do business. Eventually, those who are unwilling to be so marked will be murdered for their refusal. In that future day, Satan will have his sealed followers, but God will have His sealed witnesses. This seal of the living God is an external mark.

The seal will also be a moral badge. These people are described as "servants of God" in Revelation 7:3. They have not bowed to the Antichrist but have devoted themselves sincerely to God.

In Joel 2:28-32, the prophet Joel seems to coordinate the judgments of the last days with a special endowment of the Holy Spirit, saying, ". . . I will pour out my spirit on all flesh; your sons and your daughters shall prophesy, your old men shall dream dreams, your young men shall see visions . . ." Therefore, if a man has the seal of God upon him, he has the power, unction, and presence of the Holy Spirit in his life.

It is hard to imagine the impact 144,000 Spirit-filled Jews might have on their world. Their "pentecostal" power would enable them to have great courage and bravery as they give witness to the Word and testimony to salvation in Jesus Christ. A genuine, devout converted Jew puts a Gentile to shame in his bold witness for Christ. Twelve Spirit-filled Jews turned their world upside down. Imagine the magnitude of the revival that will take place during the Tribulation.

## Who Are Those Who Are Sealed?

Without question, Revelation 7:3 is one of the most important and, at the same time, controversial verses in the entire Bible. Before we identify who these "servants of God" are, let's identify who they are not.

They are not the same people as the multitude mentioned in verse 9. These sealed "servants" are numbered; they are from Israel; they are on earth; they are preserved in tribulation and have not yet been rewarded. The multitude is unnumbered; it is from every nation, kindred, people, and tongue; it is in heaven; it is removed from tribulation and has palms and robes.

The "sealed" are not the church. The church is already in heaven, raptured between chapters 3 and 4. We see them in the presence of the elders as two distinct groups. No error confuses interpretation and destroys the unity of the Bible like substituting the church for Israel.

They are not the Seventh-Day Adventists. Adventists believe these 144,000 are members of their church who are found observing the Jewish sabbath when the Lord comes back again, and thus they are raptured up to glory. In order for this to be true, every such Seventh-Day Adventist would have to be Jewish and from one of the twelve tribes.

They are also not the Jehovah's Witnesses who are all striving to become one of the so-called "elect." It was formerly taught that all Jehovah's Witnesses were among this number, but their ranks have since swelled to more than 144,000 people. Now they teach that the 144,000 are "overcomers." Their doctrine is a system of works based upon a misapplication of this verse.

These 144,000 are ALL of the tribes of the children of Israel. The Holy Spirit actually names the names of the tribes so that there will be no doubt. Their mention in Revelation 7:4-8 refutes the idea that the tribes of Israel are lost.

It also destroys the system of interpretation called "Anglo-Israelism," or "British Israelism," which holds that the ten tribes of the northern kingdom of Israel, carried away during the Assyrian conquest, later escaped from that country, wandered to Europe, and settled in the British Isles. Thus, the British people, according to this view, are the true Israelites and all the blessings that Israel had in the Old Testament now belong to Britain. The United States is included in this theory because of our predominantly British ancestry. This view also separates Jews and Israelites. They say the Jews are descendants of Judah, the only tribe in Palestine during our Lord's ministry on earth. These Jews alone were responsible for the crucifixion of Christ and a curse has rested on them ever since.

Someone has rightly concluded that this system of interpretation denies the redemptive work of Jesus Christ, causing people to rest in their lineage for salvation instead of the atoning blood of Jesus Christ.

Perhaps the present location of the twelve tribes is known only to God, but He can certainly call them back when He chooses.

This matter of the identity of the tribes is significant. This is only one of 29 lists of the 12 tribes to be found in the Bible. However, rather than mention each tribe that is listed, it would do well for us to note the exceptions.

The first exception is Judah, the tribe from which Jesus Christ comes. Judah is mentioned first, instead of Reuben, who is the oldest son of Jacob. Reuben forfeited his birthright because of his sin with his father's concubine (1 Chronicles 5:1-2).

Secondly, Dan's tribe is not listed. The son of Rachel's handmaid, Bilhah, Dan is referred to in Genesis 49:17 as a "serpent." In Deuteronomy 33:22, he is called a "lion." The only other person in Scripture referred to by both of these titles is Satan. There are some who think the Antichrist will come from the tribe of Dan because of the idolatries of that tribe recorded in Scripture. In Ezekiel 48, we learn that God does give Dan a portion of land in the extreme north, farther from the temple than any other tribe.

Levi is the third exception. Levi originally had no geographical region assigned to his descendants in the promised land, so his name does not usually appear on the lists of the 12 tribes. Rather, they were given particular cities in all the various tribal areas. In this list, Levi is mentioned, perhaps as taking the place of Dan, since this is a list of the servants of God who have been sealed for ministry. Who would belong on such a list more than Levi!

The fourth exception to note is the omission of Ephraim. Manasseh, one of Joseph's two sons, is mentioned, while Joseph takes Ephraim's place. Like Dan, Ephraim was guilty of idolatry. Perhaps Joseph is mentioned here to show that all the tribes are together again.

## Why Are They Sealed?

They are sealed for protection. Just as God kept the three Hebrew children alive in the fire (Daniel 3:1-26), so these sealed Hebrews will be kept alive and protected throughout the time of "Jacob's trouble." In Revelation 9:4, specific instruction is given that the fifth blown trumpet is to harm only "those men who do not have the seal of God on their foreheads."

They are also sealed for power, as they will be empowered to preach the Gospel to their world. The result will only be explainable in terms of the Holy Spirit and His infilling. The great multitude described in the last half of chapter 7 are evidently the product of these great evangelists preaching the Gospel of Jesus Christ.

Finally, they are sealed for promise. They are to enter the kingdom at the end of the Tribulation to reign with Christ and His glorified church. They are kept alive through the Tribulation in order to be present when the millennium begins, thus fulfilling God's covenant promises to His people.

The most obvious, most important message derived from this passage would have to be that EVEN IN JUDGMENT, GOD IS MERCIFUL. Each judgment of God, from Noah to the judgment of God's own Son in our behalf, reveals the mercy of God.

1. Read Ezekiel 9:3-4 and note what you learn about "setting a mark on the foreheads." Why was the mark placed there?

2. Read Ezekiel 8:6-18, then list what you see going on with the house of Israel.

What was God's response in verse 18?

3. What do Numbers 14:18 and Deuteronomy 5:9-10 reveal about God?

About His judgments?

4. Now read Deuteronomy 5:29 and record what God says there.

5. Summarize what you have learned about God's judgments.

6. What does Revelation 14:1 reveal about a seal or mark?

Who bears this mark?

7. Read 2 Corinthians 1:21-22, Ephesians 1:13, and Ephesians 4:30. Then record what you learn about the "seal."

8. What do you think that seal represents in your life?

9. Read the instruction found in Galatians 5:16. Write it out.

Read Galatians 5:22-24. What do these verses represent in relationship to the instruction above?

10. Acts 6:8 introduces us to a disciple named Stephen, against whom false charges were made and who then had to appear before the Council to give a defense. What does Acts 6:15 say about the way he looked?

11. Exodus 34:35 reports something unique about the face of Moses after he had been in God's presence. What is it?

12. From these two Scriptures, what might the "seal of the Living God," spoken of in Revelation 7:2, look like?



13. What can you learn about the mercy of God, even in judgment, from the following Scriptures?

The account of Noah in Genesis 6-8?



The account of Sodom and Gomorrah in Genesis 18:16-33?



The account of Rahab in Joshua 2:1-25, 6:16-17?



14. Read Psalm 33:18, Psalm 86:5 and Psalm 100:5. Record what you learn about the Lord's mercy.



15. Has the Lord extended mercy to you?



When? Did you deserve it?

Why did He extend mercy to you?

16. Read Galatians 5:22-24 again, and write out what the Holy Spirit reveals to you about the character change brought about because God extended mercy to you.

DID YOU KNOW?

Throughout Scripture, the number 12 is often associated with Israel. The Jewish high priest wore a breastplate with 12 precious stones representing the 12 tribes. On the table of showbread in the temple were 12 holy loaves representing the 12 tribes of Israel. In the great city, the New Jerusalem, are 12 gates and on each is written the name of one of the tribes. In Matthew 19:28, we are told of a future day when the 12 apostles will be seated on 12 thrones judging the 12 tribes of Israel.

# Tribulation Harvest

In this lesson we will see a passage that contains
seeds of encouragement for hurting people.

The multitude spoken of in these verses has experienced not
only suffering and death, but also the comfort and beauty
John describes in this priceless picture of the final state of the
blessed dead.

I. **Who Is This Multitude?** • Revelation 7:9
   A. It is not the church
   B. It is the Gentiles saved during tribulation
   C. It represents fulfillment of prophecy (Matthew 24:14)

II. **Conditions of the Multitude** • Revelation 7:9-17
   A. Status
   B. Salvation
   C. Safety
   D. Singing
   E. Service
   F. Shepherding

III. **Judgment in Heaven**
   A. Judgment seat of Christ
   B. Great White Throne judgment
   C. Is there a second chance?

IV. **A Word of Encouragement**

Throughout all the ages of the church, there have been certain passages that have been a blessing to people who are hurting. Revelation 7: 9-17 presents a picture of the state of the blessed dead. Here, John uses a phrase he repeats several times in the Book of Revelation. The phrase translated "all nations, peoples, and tongues" (v. 9) is used to picture the multitude in heaven, much like the gathering of people in great cities and cosmopolitan churches of John's day.

## Who Is This Multitude?

We can know, first of all, that it is not the church. We have noted earlier that the church is already in heaven, having gotten there between chapters 3 and 4, and is represented by the 24 elders sitting, not standing, around the throne. We can further note several distinctive differences between this group gathered in the last part of the seventh chapter and the group of believers gathered in the fourth chapter.

First of all, the church is kept from the Great Tribulation, but this group is said to have come "out of the Great Tribulation" (v. 14). The people of the "multitude" wear white robes, whereas the church is dressed in white raiment. The multitude is standing; the church is seated. The multitude is uncrowned; the church wears crowns. Those who have already gathered have harps and vials, while the people of the multitude are carrying palms. Earlier, we noted that the church sang a "new song," while these people are crying out with a loud voice.

As we study the Book of Revelation, we need to remember that there is no single group that encompasses everything that is going on until the end of the book, when everyone comes together for eternity. Until that time, there are representatives of all the various states of God's work—the Jews, the church, and the multitude of the saints, who are basically the Gentiles who have been saved during the Tribulation period. They have been won to Christ by the 144,000 Jewish evangelists, as we learned in Revelation 6.

The majority of saints in the Tribulation period will die as martyrs. Some will be killed in earthquakes, some will die during war and pestilence, others will be the objects of special persecution by the world ruler. They will be "hounded to death," as the Jews were during World War II. They will not be allowed to worship Christ, but because they will not worship the Beast, they will be under sentence of death. The result will be thousands upon thousands martyred during the Tribulation.

The people of the multitude, then, are those who have come out of the Great Tribulation and have washed their robes white with the blood of the Lamb. Scripture says there will be so many they cannot be counted.

In this harvest of souls that is the result of the work of the 144,000 Jewish evangelists, we are seeing fulfilled the prophecy contained in Matthew 24:14: "And this Gospel of the kingdom will be preached in all the world as a witness to all the nations, and then the end will come." You may hear people say that the Rapture cannot occur until the whole world has heard the Gospel; therefore, we need to preach the Gospel to every creature so that the "last person to be saved" is brought into the kingdom, at which time Jesus will return for His church. This cannot be true. If there is anything that has yet to happen before Christ's return, there is no such thing as the "imminent return" of Jesus Christ. There is not one thing that needs to be done before He returns. He could come tonight!

The command to take the Gospel into the whole world is certainly pressing upon every generation, but the condition of the Gospel going to the whole world is a condition not of the Rapture, but of the second coming of Christ. As we examine this great multitude in heaven, we see people who have been won to Christ after the Rapture has occurred.

The Gospel message must be taken everywhere. Thus, the prophecy referred to in Matthew 24:14 is fulfilled, not in our time, but in their time. Perhaps radio, television, the printed page, satellites, and all the technology we have now will be used during that day. The Gospel will go everywhere and people will be saved, and then the end will come.

## Conditions of the Multitude

The first thing we notice about the multitude is their status. It is one of power and honor before the Almighty God, because we see this group standing before the throne and before the Lamb, whereas the church is seated.

In verse 9 and verses 13-14, we notice that the people of the multitude have made their robes white because they were washed in the blood of the Lamb. This is a reference to their salvation and probably relates to Revelation 6:11. In the Scriptures, when people are referred to as being clothed in white, it can mean one of two things: either they have been washed and clothed through salvation in the righteousness of Christ or they have clothed themselves in righteousness as believers. There is both an inward and an outward righteousness which is usually distinguished by the use of this figurative language regarding white clothes. In the Greek, the phrase used here is "white stoles." The Greek word translated "stoles" refers to an outer garment worn to reflect dignity, grace, distinction, and beauty.

Third, we notice the safety of the multitude. There are two indications of this condition: the reference to palm branches in their hands (v. 9) and the statement that God will dwell among them (v. 15).

Palms were a part of the celebration of the Jewish Feast of Tabernacles, during which the Jews, for a period of time, lived in booths which they constructed. They also carried palm branches to remind them of the time when God delivered them from the terrible slavery of Egypt. There are many other occasions recorded in Scripture when the Jews used palm branches as a reminder of deliverance from tribulation, trial, and difficulty. Palm branches represented celebration. Here in Revelation 7, the people of the multitude are excited and thrilled because of what God has done for them. Theirs is a celebration of joy!

The phrase in verse 15 regarding God dwelling with them actually means "He who sits on the throne will spread His tent over them." God's shepherding, sheltering care on their behalf is pictured in that phrase. He literally spreads His tent over them and they are safe at last. That's the spirit of their celebration.

Now, notice the singing of the multitude in heaven. Their song is one of praise to God for their salvation; they have come through the Great Tribulation and have arrived in heaven. They have been delivered, not just in the sense of having been taken away from the tribulation, but also in the sense that they have been enabled to conquer in the power of Christ. They have overcome! These Gentile converts are shouting to the Lord in heaven, and the song of the redeemed triggers the angelic choir.

They begin to sing in a seven-fold description of praise as they worship the One who sits on the throne (v. 12).

We also notice, in verse 15, the service of the multitude. First, there is to be singing and worship, and second, there will be service, day and night, in His temple. In the Old Testament, the privilege of serving God day and night belonged to only two types of people: the Levites and the priests. When the Gentiles were on earth, they were not allowed to enter the temple; they could not go beyond the Court of the Gentiles on pain of death. However, in this temple, the way to the presence of God is open to people of every race; all are engaged in glad, unceasing service to their God. There are no barriers, no restraints—only absolute, total openness to the throne of God. To serve day and night indicates they will not need sleep or rest, but will serve continually, with no limitations. We can see the wonderful opportunity for personal fellowship, for the Lord Himself is going to dwell with them.

Finally, in verse 16, we see the shepherding of the multitude by God Himself. Why is being shepherded so important to this group of people? Think what they have been experiencing in the Tribulation period. This provision by the Lord contrasts starkly to what they have just gone through. Because they were believers, they were starved by the Antichrist; they couldn't buy food without the mark of the Beast. The rivers were turned to blood, so there was no water to drink. What they did not have then, God is now specifically providing for them. And notice that verse 16 states they will not suffer these things "anymore." Now all the tears and sorrow of their former lives are going to be put behind them forever; God is going to wipe away the tears from their eyes (v. 7). That phrase indicates that the tears are not just wiped away, but taken out of their eyes, so that there are no more left.

It is theologically incorrect to say that there will be no more tears in heaven. If that were correct, what is God going to wipe away here? There will be tears, and Scripture records that they will be wiped away on two occasions, both related to the two judgments of God.

## Judgment in Heaven

God will wipe away the tears of the Christians for two reasons. First, at the judgment seat of Christ (2 Corinthians 5:9-10), we will weep when we realize what we could have done for Christ but didn't. Some will look back over lives that were wasted, ruined, squandered. The biggest waste is to think you can live your own life, have your fling, and then accept Christ in order to go to heaven. What a terrible thing to waste a life! What an overwhelming sense of rebellion to say that to God! God may not allow you that option. That's a sobering, awesome thought. We will also weep when we see the unsaved people we could have witnessed to, but didn't, as they perish and go to hell for eternity. Remember that the Tribulation period here on earth coincides with the judgment seat of Christ in heaven.

In Revelation 21:4, we find that God wipes away tears just after the Great White Throne judgment, when all of the unsaved appear before God and He says, "Depart from Me, for I never knew you," and they go into eternity, lost forever. After that, God wipes away the tears, ultimately and finally, of the people who are in heaven.

Some are concerned when there is talk of a great revival taking place during the Tribulation period, thinking that this represents a "second chance" at salvation for those who have refused the claims of Christ while alive on this earth before the Tribulation. There will be no second chance, no opportunity to reject Christ and then accept Him after the Rapture occurs. This reference to the multitude being saved during the Tribulation period does not refer to the people who had a chance in their lifetime to be saved but rejected Christ. 2 Thessalonians 2:10-12 indicates that the person who hears the Gospel and refuses salvation before the Tribulation will not be saved because he will be sent a strong delusion due to his "pleasure in unrighteousness."

What lie will he believe? Revelation 13 tells us it will be the lies of the Beast and the Antichrist, who fabricate the life of Christ and bring deception. Believing these deceptions, the people who have rejected the Gospel before the Tribulation will go to hell without opportunity to receive Christ. The day of grace will be over for them. There is no second chance. This is the day of salvation!

## A Word of Encouragement

The most important point in this passage is not the discouragement of people missing out on salvation; rather, it is the encouragement of recognizing that when we go through trouble, tribulation, and suffering, God understands. He takes us through it, and when we come out, He ministers to every need we have personally. This is not a ministry God waits until eternity to do for us. He is in that business today. He wants to help and encourage us because He knows what we are experiencing. He loves us and ministers to us in the midst of our tribulations.

| APPLICATION | REVELATION 7:9-17 |
| --- | --- |

1. The record of Israel contained in Nehemiah 8 relates some interesting events. In verse 1, what did the people ask Ezra, the priest, to do?

What was their reaction in verses 5-6 as the book was read?

Nehemiah 8:7-8 indicate the people had the book explained to them for what purpose?

According to Nehemiah 8:9, what was their reaction?

What was the cause of this reaction according to verses 10-12?

2. What did the people do in Nehemiah 8:15-17?

Why did they do it, according to verse 14?

How does this relate to our study this week?

3. Read John 12:12-15 and note what the people do as Jesus is coming to Jerusalem.

Why do they do this?

What does this indicate they were looking for?

4. What do Matthew 20:28 and John 20:31 reveal about the reason that Jesus came to earth?

What had to take place in order for that to be accomplished? Read John 3:14-15 and 12:32 for the answer.

5. The 23rd Psalm says "The LORD is my shepherd . . ." List the things you learn there about what a shepherd provides.

Read your list again and personalize each element. How have you experienced the Lord as your shepherd?

6. What does Hebrews 9:27 say about death and judgment?

Is there a "second chance"? What does the Scripture say?

7. Does 1 John 4:17 offer any encouragement? If so, write out how it encourages you.

8. Does Hebrews 7:25 offer any encouragement? If so, write out how it encourages you.

9. Finally, read the solemn charge recorded in 2 Timothy 4:1-4. Write out what the Holy Spirit says to you personally from these verses. What would He have you do in response to what you have learned this week? Ask Him!

DID YOU KNOW?

In Revelation 7:13-14, John is asked by one of the elders, "Who are these arrayed in white robes?" and he answers, "Sir, you know" His response in the Greek is an idiom meaning "I don't know."

# The Seventh Seal

We have unrolled the scroll, or the title-deed to the
earth, all the way to the end, and there is only one seal left.
We remove that seal in this lesson.

OUTLINE  R E V E L A T I O N  8 : 1 - 1 3

In the scroll were seven seals. We have studied the first six. Now
we learn that contained within the seventh seal are the seven
trumpet judgments. As the various trumpets sound in this chapter,
the planet is handed over to the Beast and the Devil's messiah.
The man of sin begins to take control.

I. **Four Thoughts As the Chapter Opens** • Revelation 8:1-13
   A. Silent pause
   B. Solemn preparation
   C. Saints' prayers
   D. Sinners' punishment
II. **Sounding of the First Four Trumpets** • Revelation 8:7-12
   A. A terrible ecological disaster begins
   B. Pollution of oceans
   C. Pollution of fresh water supplies
   D. The heavens and time cycles affected
III. **The Awful Announcement of What Is to Come** • Revelation 1:13
IV. **Prepared Now for the Rule of Satan**

The first few chapters of the Book of Revelation deal with the churches. These are followed by a discussion of the Tribulation period. The beginning of that Tribulation has been pictured for us by a scroll, or title-deed to the earth, upon which are the seals. Remember that these seals have been seen as the scroll has been unrolled, and each has revealed the contents of the judgments a little at a time. In essence, then, when we remove the seventh seal from the scroll, we are unraveling the remainder of the plan of God for this earth in the Book of Revelation.

As we begin our study of chapter 8, it is well to remember that the church is gone from the earth; most of the converted Jews have been martyred for their faith, and many of the Gentiles who have come to Christ as the result of the evangelism done by the 144,000 have been martyred for giving their testimony for the Lord. They are all in heaven. However, here on earth, tremendous judgment is being poured out.

The six seal judgments we have studied have given us a vision of a world that has been ruined by men. Plagues, wars, death—all have illustrated the wrath of God's judgment, brought on by mismanagement of men. Now, after the parenthesis of chapter 7, we come to the last of the seals. The encouragement of chapter 7 is over, and the world ruined by men under the seal judgments is about to become a world ruled by Satan under the trumpet judgments.

Under the seal judgments, men are horrified, and they cry out to God that the wrath of the Lamb has come. But, under the trumpet judgments we are about to study, the world will become so bad that it will be easy for Satan's man to take over. Under the trumpet judgments, men are hardened and their concern is not about the Lamb, but about the Beast who has come upon this earth.

## Four Thoughts As the Chapter Opens

First, there is a silent pause (Revelation 8:1) that indicates the horror of what is about to happen. There is a period of silence—notice, it is in heaven, not on earth. There is a day coming when all the earth will be silent before God. But the heavens have been filled with the noises of worship; the choirs have been singing, and the angels have been praising God. The seven-sealed book is completely open, and the breaking of the seventh seal brings a strange hush, foreshadowing a solemn event. Judgment is about to come upon the land. It is the breathless silence that precedes the storm. All of heaven is waiting to see what will happen.

First of all, it is a silence of awe and expectancy, but it is also an ominous silence of foreboding. One half hour, in the right set of circumstances, can seem an eternity!

Then there is the solemn preparation of Revelation 8:2. The seven angels in this verse have the task of announcing the execution of judgment through the sounding of trumpets, heralding the great, final intervention of God in judgment. These are solemn moments in heaven because the judgments about to occur are terrible. They are the awful judgments prophesied in both the Old and New Testaments. These angels have a very important role in the unfolding events. Verse 6 indicates they had to prepare themselves to blow the trumpets. Recognizing that He is about to bring judgment, we come to the third point. Verses 3-5 reveal the saints' prayers, which are not necessarily positive prayers. Rather, they are imprecations against the earth. Possibly, Revelation 6:9-10 is the prayer that is referred to here. The saints are praying that God will go into action and vindicate His people. Remember, these who are praying are the people killed for their faith, martyred for their Lord. Now they are in heaven, apparently having some knowledge of the terrible wickedness upon the earth. They pray, "How long, O Lord, holy and true, until you judge and avenge our blood on those who dwell on the earth?" We can know that this is the nature of their prayer because immediately after their prayers ascend, the judgment descends! As soon as they pray, their prayer is answered.

The altar from which the angel filled the censer with fire represents the place of judgment; the fire represents the judgment of God upon sin. We are told that the fire around the altar is now emptied upon the earth, poured out as a judgment. The Tribulation period is over, and the great day of God's wrath is being poured out. The saints' prayer is about to be answered in the sinners' punishment. Revelation 8:6-13 begins the record of the sounding of the first four trumpets.

## Sounding the First Four Trumpets

Revelation 11:15 tells us that the trumpet judgments appear just before the second coming of Christ. Notice that the voices in heaven were saying, "The kingdoms of this world have become the kingdoms of our Lord, and of His Christ . . . ." We begin looking at the last section of the book of Revelation, just before Christ comes to this earth to set up His kingdom, as we study the trumpet judgments.

The first trumpet is sounded in Revelation 8:7. We would have no more reason to interpret these passages symbolically than we do to interpret symbolically the plagues of the book of Exodus, for instance. Therefore, literally, when the first trumpet sounds, hail and fire are mingled with blood and cast upon the earth, and a third of the trees, along with all the green grass, is burned up. With the sounding of the first trumpet there is going to begin a terrible ecological devastation of the earth, in which a third of all vegetation will be destroyed. It is a bleak picture. We can't understand what it will do to the balance of nature. But our responsibility is to believe it, not understand it.

As the second trumpet sounds (vv. 8-9), a great mountain burning with fire is cast into the sea. With these judgments that are happening upon the earth, we can expect that many things will happen that have never happened before in the history of the world. That is why the judgments will be so awesome. We can see that, literally, the sea will become blood and one-third of all sea life will die. There will also be the destruction of one-third of all the shipping of the world. The far-reaching implications of these judgments is beyond our understanding. Someone has reasoned that the oceans occupy about three-fourths of the earth's surface, so the extent of this judgment will be staggering. The pollution of the water and the death of so many sea creatures will vastly affect the balance of life in the ocean. This will happen to one-third of the salt water bodies of the world.

When the second trumpet has been silenced, the third trumpet sounds in (vv. 10-11). The judgment of the third trumpet affects the fresh water supplies, which will become bitter, with the result that many people will die. The instrument of judgment will be a great star which is labeled "Wormwood." There are many species of wormwood growing in Palestine. They all have a strong bitter taste and serve as a symbol of sorrow, bitterness, and calamity.

We can see from these verses that there is a meteoric phenomenon which takes place. A literal star or meteor hurtling through space approaches the earth. Sweeping along the surface of the earth, it turns one-third of the water of the earth into a deadly poisonous liquid. It affects the rivers, springs, and wells. A similar event happened on March 21, 1823, when a volcanic explosion on the Aleutian islands caused the water to become so bitter it was unfit for use. God uses what He creates to affect His ends!

The fourth trumpet sounds in Revelation 8:12-13, and the next judgment affects the sun, moon, stars, and the uniformity of day and night. Can you imagine the chaos on the earth when the sun, moon, and stars will be smitten to such an extent that one-third of them will be out of kilter, and, apparently, the 24-hour cycle we have come to know will be shortened to a 16-hour cycle?

As John records the sounding of the fourth trumpet and its results, he hears "an angel flying through the midst of heaven" (v. 13).

## The Awful Announcement of What Is to Come

The word translated "angel" should be "eagle." This "eagle" is flying through the midst of heaven, "saying with a loud voice, 'woe, woe, woe ... ' " The sounding of the fourth trumpet is simply a warning that there are three trumpets of judgment to come. Woe be unto the inhabitants of the earth! These last three trumpets are going to bring a new quality and degree of divine displeasure, with disaster as its consequence.

We shall see the first woe, locusts, in Revelation 9:3. Verses 14-17 will reveal the second woe—the four angels of the Euphrates river and their armies. Revelation 11 reveals the plagues of the two witnesses as they smite the earth. The culmination of it all will come in Revelation 13, with the handing over of the earth to the Beast.

## Prepared Now for the Rule of Satan

All of the events of the Tribulation are simply preparations for the world to be handed over to Satan for his rule.

Let's consider the scenario. Imagine for a moment what

you would feel if you had experienced firsthand what we have described prophetically in this lesson. You have lost friends and loved ones because of this judgment. Devastation has totally taken out some cities and towns where your loved ones lived, and there is no telephone communication across the nation. The news is filled with unpredictable and unexpected tragedy. On the late news, word begins to spread that someone has come to the front and announced his ability to deal with these overwhelming calamities. He describes his hope and his vision and talks of the miraculous powers that have been given him. He will announce his plans on a later television broadcast. Would you be in front of your television that night? You would! All of life's other concerns would be laid aside. Every person would be sitting spellbound, hoping against hope that this man's intentions would be realized. The Scriptures say that when that happens, the Beast, the man of sin, the Devil's christ, will step to the front and galvanize the world behind his leadership, leading them with promises he never intends to keep. His final control of all the world will ultimately lead to the gigantic battle we know as Armageddon.

In the seal judgments we see the world ruined by man. In the trumpet judgments, we see the world ruled by Satan. But by the time we get to the end of the trumpet judgments, we will see the world reclaimed by Christ! The earth must go through the cycle, because that is what the Bible says. The good news is that we, as individuals, will not have to experience it. We can "go up" at the end of chapter 3. As we read and study this Book of Revelation, may it be all the motivation we need to invite the Lord Jesus Christ into our lives as Savior and Lord. Accept Him while there is still opportunity.

| APPLICATION | REVELATION 8:1-13 |

1. Read Numbers 10:2-10, Judges 3:26-30, and Nehemiah 4:1-21. Record what you learn about the reasons for the sounding of trumpets in these passages.

How does that compare to Revelation 8?

2. What "trumpet" do you think God is sounding for us right now in the churches?

How are you responding?

3. Joshua 6:1-16 gives another account of the blowing of a trumpet. As you read it, record the important points and the purpose of blowing the trumpet.

4. Jesus Himself predicted at the Mount of Olives the events which will be fulfilled in Revelation 8. Read Luke 21:25-26 and note any points of similarity.

5. Worship is defined as acknowledging the "worth-ship" of God. As you read the following Scriptures, list what you learn about the worthiness of God:

Psalm 119:142

Isaiah 47:4

Psalm 89:14

Romans 5:8

2 Timothy 2:13

Daniel 2:20

6. We have seen the phrase "solemn preparation." Is there anything we must do that relates to this? Read the following verses and write out what they reveal about your personal preparation:

Psalm 46:10

Proverbs 2:1-4

What are the results promised in Proverbs 2:5-6?

7. Read the following verses and note what you learn about the "saints' prayers." Personalize your answers.

Philippians 4:6-7

Matthew 6:9-13

1 Thessalonians 5:16-18

8. Now look at 1 Corinthians 2:9-10, and record the promise of God that is a result of these things.

9. Finally, read Romans 8:31-39, and record the promises of God you find there.

To whom are these promises made? Read Romans 8:28.

Are you one who is "the called according to His purpose"? On what basis do you know this?

DID YOU KNOW?

As of January, 1981, there were 24,867 ocean-going merchant ships registered. Imagine the shock waves in the shipping industry if 8,289 of these ships with their valuable cargoes were suddenly destroyed. The National Geographic Society lists approximately 100 principal rivers in the world, with the Amazon, at 4,000 miles, the longest. The U.S. Geological Survey reports there are 30 large rivers in the United States. The Mississippi River, at 3,710 miles, is the longest. One-third of these major rivers and their sources will become so bitterly polluted that their drinking water will produce instant death.

# The Fifth Trumpet—Hell on Earth Part 1

In this lesson we will look at a detailed description
of the fifth trumpet judgment.

OUTLINE    R E V E L A T I O N    9 : 1 - 1 2

As we study the fifth trumpet judgment we will examine the unlocking of the pit and its effect on mankind. We will study the demon creatures that are released from the pit and see the horrors they inflict upon those who do not belong to God. We will see hell spill over on the earth during this period of Tribulation.

I. **Fitting Chapter 9 into the Book of Revelation** • Revelation 9:1-12
II. **The Unnamed Personality** • Revelation 9:1
III. **The Unlocked Pit** • Revelation 9:2
IV. **The Unleashed Power** • Revelation 9:2-6
   A. The description of the demons from the pit
   B. The damage of the demons from the pit
V. **The Unscrupulous Prince** • Revelation 9:11
VI. **God's Warning to Mankind**

Many people decide that the best way to deal with the truth that is before us in this lesson is to ignore it. They pass over chapters like this one to get to more positive messages. Any discussion of "hell" in today's ecclesiastical circles is bound to create resistance and ridicule. Some groups say that there is no hell. A typical statement was found in a *Life Magazine* article. In this article Dana McClean states, "From a Unitarian point of view, there is no heaven or hell. Theologically, such an idea is repulsive and unacceptable in the light of the moral affirmation of man."

The Bible teaches that there *is* a place called "hell." It is a literal place that is burning with fire and brimstone. In the ninth chapter of Revelation, we get just a brief glimpse of the horrors of hell, as we see it spill over on the earth during that terrible period of judgment known as the Tribulation.

## Chapter Nine and the Book of Revelation

We know from our previous studies that the next event on the prophetic calendar is the Rapture of the church to heaven. All church-age believers, both living and dead, are to be snatched off the earth and taken to heaven in advance of the actual Tribulation period.

But here on earth there will be tribulation. At the climax of the "Great Tribulation" Jesus Christ will come with his saints to fight against Satan's armies and will be victorious at the Battle of Armageddon. He will then rule in righteousness for one thousand years. At the end of this millennial reign of Christ, the Great White Throne Judgment will be experienced by every person who has rejected Christ.

In the ninth chapter of Revelation we see a continuation of that which began in chapter 5. In the fifth chapter we see God seated on His throne with a book in His hand. This book represents the many judgments that God is going to bring upon this earth. The only one found worthy to open the seals and reveal the content of the book is Jesus Christ, the Lion of the tribe of Judah. As each seal is removed, an additional portion of the scroll is made visible and another judgment is poured out.

The seventh seal reveals the seven trumpet judgments, and the seventh trumpet judgment reveals the seven bowl judgments. It is correct to say that the seals include all that is to happen in the Tribulation period.

As we come to the ninth chapter, we have studied the first six seal judgments. In them we have seen that in just a few days, God has taken this globe and in cataclysmic measures has ripped apart those things that had caused it to be stabilized. We are now working our way through the seventh seal judgment.

If someone were to go to all the prisons and jails of our land and turn loose the murderers and rapists and child molesters, we would not have a situation as bad as the one described here.

## The Unnamed Personality

Like the imagery of the third trumpet, we are made to see a star falling from heaven. This star is a human personality. The pronouns "he" and "him" are used of this star in verses one and two. Who is this unnamed personality who has fallen from heaven? It is none other than Satan himself. In the events described in this section, Satan is fulfilling his self-disclosed purpose. He is bringing all the pressure and evil upon this earth that hell can devise. During the time described in these verses, Satan is given permission by God to let loose the demons of hell for a season. He is allowed to open the prison house of the evil spirits and turn them loose.

If we study the Greek text, we would see that the perfect tense is used to describe the Fall. Literally the text says, "I saw a star having fallen from heaven." In other words, when John saw the star, it had already fallen.

The Bible teaches that Satan was kicked out of heaven on two separate occasions. The first predates the creation of man (Luke 10:18 and Isaiah 14:12). The second expulsion of Satan from heaven is described for us in Revelation 12:7-9. (Chapter 12, according to many scholars, actually fits within the context of chapter 9.)

## The Unlocked Pit

Satan is now given permission by God to take the lid off the bottomless pit and let all the creatures out who have been incarcerated from the beginning. The Greek word for "pit" is *abussos* or abyss. This suggests an image of a vast depth approached by a shaft, whose top, or mouth, is covered. The description of this place in Dante's *Inferno*, with its narrowing circles winding down to the central shaft, is somewhat similar. It is descriptive of the deep pit or place where evil angels were bound in chains after the Fall. By looking at other Scripture we can learn more about the pit:

1. It is a place dreaded by the demons (Luke 8:26-31). The word "deep" used here is *abussos*. The demons were talking about the bottomless pit. They did not want to be confined.
2. It is a place where fallen angels are retained (Jude 6).
3. It is the place where Jesus Christ preached in between His death and His resurrection. He actually went to this place and proclaimed victory over death to the fallen angels (Romans 10:7; I Peter 3:18-19).
4. It is a place which is ultimately controlled by Jesus Christ. He has the keys and He gave them to Satan (Revelation 1:18).
5. It is the place where Satan will be bound for a thousand years (Revelation 20:1-3).

## The Unleashed Power

The result of unlocking the pit is the unleashing of the soot of hell. The blackness of evil and a spiritual plague of great proportions breaks out upon the earth fueled by the work of millions of demons. The creatures that ascend from the bottomless pit are locust-like creatures. Who are these locusts? These are not real locusts of the insect variety. We can come to this conclusion by looking at several factors. The locusts of Revelation 9 do not eat vegetation (v. 4); have a king over them (v. 11—this king is Satan himself. Proverbs 30:27 says that real locusts have no king); cannot be real locusts because Exodus 10:14 says that after the plagues of Egypt, no such locusts would ever be seen again.

## The Description of the Demons from the Pit

How would you describe demons so that people would be able to picture them? In Revelation 9 we see them described as having a likeness to several kinds of animals: lions, horses, scorpions, and men.

As horses (v. 7) we see them as imperial creatures. In Oriental culture the horse was a picture of royal power; it went forth to battle. Nothing was more powerful than a horse carrying his master into battle.

They are shown as invulnerable creatures (v. 7) with crowns on their heads. These creatures are viewed as victorious in their quest and invulnerable to the attacks of the enemy.

The face of men (v. 7) implies that they are intelligent creatures.

They are described as having hair as the hair of women. This would make them intriguing creatures, because in this culture nothing was considered more seductive than a woman's hair. These demons are repulsive in much of their appearance; yet at the same time, they are seductive, sensual, and intriguing.

They are inhuman creatures (v. 8) having teeth as the teeth of lions.

They are indestructible creatures with their breastplates as of iron (v. 9).

They are impressive creatures (v. 9) having the sound of their wings as the sound of chariots with many horses.

What would a swarm of demons be like when released from hell where they have been chained for thousands of years? It would be impossible to understand this whole scene apart from descriptive terms like the ones in this passage.

## The Damage of the Demons from the Pit

What will be the result of countless demons running unchecked throughout the earth during this time? It will be an awful experience for those who are left to endure it. Among other things the experience will be:

1. Painful (v. 10): The sting of scorpions is not lethal, but it is one of the most painful stings known to man. The poison that enters the system as the result of such a sting literally sets the nerve center on fire.
2. Protracted (v. 10): This evil will be stretched out for 150 days (5 months, which is the life span of a locust).
3. Personal (v. 4): The only people these demons are allowed to sting are those who do not belong to God.
4. Perpetual (v. 6): This activity will never cease and death cannot provide escape. Even though men will seek to die and suicide will be attempted, apparently death will not be possible.

## The Unscrupulous Prince

The Devil is the king over all these demons. Under his direction and at his bidding, these demons go to and fro upon the earth to sting every person who is not marked with the seal of God. The two names given to Satan in this verse both mean "destroyer." But this is not the end. Verse 12 warns that there are two woes to come.

## God's Warning to Mankind

This chapter of Revelation is a warning chapter. Everything that is pictured here as taking place on earth is in reality a small glimpse of an eternal hell. This reminds us that hell is a place of fire and smoke, of pain and of crying. Hell is a place where one cannot die. But let us leave this gruesome study with a word of pleading from the Lord: "As I live," says the Lord God, "I have no pleasure in the death of the wicked, but that the wicked turn from his way and live. Turn, turn from your evil ways! For why should you die, O house of Israel?" (Ezekiel 33:11).

---

**APPLICATION    REVELATION    9 : 1 - 12**

---

1. When the word "hell" is mentioned, what pictures and adjectives come to your mind?

2. We are told by many in our society that there is no hell. The Bible, however, tells us otherwise. Look at each Scripture to see what you learn about hell.

Matthew 5:22, 29, 30

Matthew 10:28

Matthew 13:41-42

Revelation 1:18


3. Satan is named as the star that John saw fall from heaven. In Scripture Satan is given many names. These names describe his character and purpose. Look at the following Scriptures to see what they reveal about him.

Psalm 109:6 and Revelation 12:10


1 Peter 5:8


Revelation 12:9


Matthew 13:19


John 8:44


Matthew 9:34


Ephesians 4:27

4. In Revelation 9:11 we find Satan called Abaddon or Apollyon. Do you remember what these names mean?

5. From our study and the Scripture you read, what is Satan's purpose?

6. Can Satan act apart from the permission of God? How do you support your answer? (Job 1:6-12; 2:2-6; Luke 22:31)

7. What did we discover as the purpose of the pit? (Jude 6; Revelation 20:1-3)

Are all demons bound in this place? Explain your answer.

8. Why do you think God bound some demons in the pit and let others free to roam the earth?

9. What are three reasons given in this lesson to prove these creatures were not real locusts?

10. Why did God choose the imagery He did to describe these demon creatures?

11. The demons from the pit were described in several ways. Give the significance of each likeness:

like horses:

as wearing crowns of gold:

like faces of men:

having hair like the hair of women:

having teeth like lions:

breastplates of iron:

the sound of chariots with many horses running to battle:

12. These demons will do untold damage. Describe what the experience will be like.

13. How and where do you see the work of demons today?

14. Who will experience their torment?

15. How will the demons know who to touch and who to pass over?

16. How did this lesson make you feel? Are you sure that you are a child of God and will never experience the pain of hell? If not, confess your sin and believe on the name of the Lord Jesus Christ. There is salvation in no one else; ". . . for there is no other name under heaven given among men by which we must be saved" (Acts 4:12).

DID YOU KNOW:

Did you know that there are over 600 warnings in the Bible about judgment and evil? Every judgment recorded in the Bible was proclaimed through a warning to those who would be judged. When God is about to act, He always speaks to his servant to tell him what He is about to do! Therefore, no one is without excuse, for God has given us the Law, the prophets, His Word, and His Son to warn us.

# The Sixth Trumpet – Hell on Earth Part 2

In this lesson we will look at the sixth trumpet judgment. We will see the destruction it causes and its effects upon mankind.

Revelation 9:13-21 describes the sixth trumpet judgment, which is also the second woe judgment. It is a continued unfolding of life on the earth after the church and the Holy Spirit have been removed. The judgment of God upon those who have rejected Him accelerates.

I. **The Demand to Judge** • Revelation 9:13-15
   A. The tools of God's judgment are prescribed by the demand
   B. The time of God's judgment is prescribed by the demand
   C. The target of God's judgment is prescribed by the demand
II. **The Details of the Judgment** • Revelation 9:16-19
III. **The Description of the Judged** • Revelation 9:18-21
   A. Their worship
   B. Their works
      1. Murders
      2. Sorceries
      3. Fornication
      4. Thefts
IV. **Conclusion**

101

We have said that the next event on the prophetic church calendar is the Rapture of the church. We believe in the pre-Tribulational, premillennial Rapture of the church. Before the Tribulation breaks up in its official form, the church of Jesus Christ will be caught out of this earth. We can know that the church will not experience the Tribulation because "There is therefore now no condemnation to those who are in Christ Jesus . . ." (Romans 8:1). There is no judgment if we know the Lord.

If you are not a Christian, everything in the book of Revelation from chapter 9 on is a message to you about the awful things that will happen after the church is gone. The only way to escape the judgment and wrath of God is to be saved and go with the church when it is raptured out of this world. If you choose to wait until after the church is gone to receive the Lord, if you are waiting to see if these prophecies are true, Scripture states that you will be sent a strong delusion and you will not be able to believe. You will then go to hell.

### The Demand to Judge

The voice in verse 13 comes from the altar of incense in heaven. This is the place where the prayers of the saints have been offered. We have been introduced to those prayers on two occasions. The first is in Revelation 6:9-11. Here we see these martyred saints asking God to avenge them, but we see God telling them that the time has not yet come. As we progress to chapter 9 we understand that the prayers of the saints are being answered.

The second occasion where we have seen prayers of the saints being offered is Revelation 8:3. What are these prayers? The prayers of these saints who have lost their lives for their faith are imprecatory prayers. They are asking God when He will judge the earth. God never tells us that their prayers are wrong. Chapter 9 is the answer to those prayers. It is time for judgment to begin.

### The Tools of God's Judgment Are Prescribed by the Demand

There are two kinds of angels in the Bible. We are introduced to the good angels in the seventh chapter (Revelation 7:1). These good angels stand at the extremities of the earth and are restraining the forces of evil.

The angels mentioned in Revelation 9:13 are evil angels

localized at the river Euphrates, and they are releasing the forces of evil upon the whole earth. There is no record in the Bible of any good angels ever being bound or restrained. Doctor John Walvoord writes, ". . . the four angels bound in the Euphrates River are evil angels who are loosed on the occasion of the sounding of the sixth trumpet in order to execute this judgment. It is another instance of the loosing of wicked angels similar to the release of the demonic locusts earlier in the fifth trumpet."

The Euphrates River is the most important river mentioned in the Bible. It flows from the Armenian Mountains to the Persian Gulf and is 1780 miles long. It flows from Eden. We see this river mentioned again in Revelation 16:12: "Then the sixth angel poured out his bowl on the great river Euphrates, and its water was dried up, so that the way of the kings from the East might be prepared." The Babylon of Revelation 17-18 is also situated at the Euphrates River.

## The Time of God's Judgment Is Prescribed by the Demand

The angels are loosed and they are to do something special. All they are to do is in God's plan and program. The four evil angels at the Euphrates River are prepared to judge at a specific time. They have been given the hour, the day, the month, and the year for their destruction of one-third of the earth's remaining population. The expression, "an hour, and a day, and a month, and a year" does not designate the duration of their activity but rather the appointed time of their activity. At the exact second, at the exact moment in God's calendar, this judgment will be let loose on the earth. We must remember that we do not have the date – God does! It is in the sovereign plan of God and it is only known by Him.

## The Target of God's Judgment Is Prescribed by the Demand

Who has been targeted by the Lord for this judgment? Revelation 9:15 says that it is "a third of mankind." If we remember from our previous lessons, we will recall that one-fourth of the world's population has already been slain (Revelation 6:8).

With this judgment of chapter 9, one-third of the remaining inhabitants are killed. If you do the calculations you will find that this leaves only one-half of the original number of persons alive on the earth. Not since The Great Flood has such a substantial proportion of the earth's population come under God's righteous judgment.

## The Details of the Judgment

"And the number of the army of the horsemen were two hundred thousand thousand: and I heard the number of them" (9:16 KJV).

How many people does that add up to? The answer is two hundred million. Some believe that since this phrase is used to describe a great host of innumerable quantity, it is not a literal number. One passage that is cited as an illustration is Revelation 5:11. Others have taken this army to be an army of demons since the weapons are fire, smoke, and brimstone (Revelation 9:17). This seems like the answer. There is, however, another possible solution to the identity of this massive army. In Revelation 16:12 we see the sixth angel pouring out his bowl on the Euphrates river and the water being dried up. This was to prepare the way of the kings from the east. Revelation 9:16 and Revelation 16:12 seem to be linked. In both passages we see the sixth angel initiating the action. Some expositors believe the bowl and the trumpet judgments overlap. Perhaps these judgments occur in more rapid succession than we think. If Revelation 16:12 is the fulfillment of this judgment, then we know this judgment is to be carried out by the armies of the East. Obviously, this would denote China and her confederated nations. Could the Chinese assemble such a massive army? If this army was assembled, could such a number of troops be moved across the continent to the arena of battle? Recently it has been revealed that Chinese soldiers are at work inside Pakistani held Kasmir on a road that would give the Chinese troops in Tibet a shortcut to the Subcontinent. India has called the Chinese roadbuilding a threat to peace in Asia. When this road is completed it will make possible the rapid movement of millions of Chinese troops into the Middle East. It will literally pave the way for John's prophecy to be fulfilled and the way of the kings of the East will be prepared.

Since nothing in John's day was known about our modern weapons, John would have had to use terms that would be symbolic.

These warriors are declared to have breastplates of fire and of jacinth and brimstone. The heads of the horses are compared to heads of lions out of whose mouths fire, smoke, and brimstone issue. The 19th verse says that the power is in their mouths and in their tails. Their tails are said to be like serpents, and even the tails have heads with which they can hurt men. Note that the terms "lions," "horses," and "serpents" all speak of deadly force. Verse 18 adds the dimensions of fire, smoke, and brimstone, which would also fit into the modern description of war. This could describe full scale military war with nuclear weapons and destruction. Nuclear war could certainly kill one-third of the world's population.

## The Description of the Judged

After reading of such awful judgment upon the earth, one would think that any who went through this judgment and escaped with their lives would be falling down before God with repentance and pleas for mercy. But their hearts are hardened and they respond to the judgment of God with added rebellion. We will look at how Revelation 9:20-21 describe them.

## Their Worship

These hardened pagans are worshiping materialism, the works of their own hands . . . idols of money, jewelry and possessions. Note the descending value of the gods they serve: gold, silver, brass, stone and wood. Since demon worship goes hand in hand with idolatry, it is no surprise to see people worshiping devils. There will be much religion practiced at this time, but it will be false religion.

## Their Works

What people believe determines what they do. Out of one's belief system a lifestyle is developed. Verse 21 tells us of four sins that will be especially rampant during this period.

MURDERS—Someone has said that wherever the Gospel is unknown, human life is cheap. It seems pagans have no problem with the taking of human life if it serves their purpose. Violent murders will be very common during this Tribulation period.

Over a century ago, Joseph Seiss, the author of *The Apocalypse*, predicted on the basis of Revelation 9:21 that capital punishment would have been largely abolished by the time of the Tribulation. He saw the day when murderers would be spared punishment because society, rather than the individual, would be held responsible for their crimes.[2]

SORCERIES—The Greek word for sorceries is *pharmakia*,

which means "pharmacy" and refers to the practice of the occult accompanied by the use of drugs. In Revelation 22:15, sorcerers are classed with dogs, murderers, fornicators and idolaters, and we are told that they have no place in the heavenly city.

FORNICATION—*Porneia* is nothing less than rampant immorality. "Porneia" refers to all kinds of sexual activity outside of the bonds of married love. When divine restraint is withdrawn, human passions will break loose and morality will be discarded in favor of liberty and "free love."

THEFTS—With all laws relaxed and with the mutual respect for each other's rights almost gone, greed will be the great motivator as those who survive the war try to prey each other. This will no doubt include burglaries and armed robberies as well as embezzlement and fraud (see Revelation 22:18).

## Conclusion

It is a solemn thing to realize that even judgment like that which we have just described will have no effect upon hardened, unregenerate man. Twice we are told that those who experience the wrath of God do not repent. Why? Man without God is hardened because of his rebellion against God. Only the Gospel through the working of the Holy Spirit can change that heart of stone and turn it into a heart of flesh. Sin paralyzes a person. It makes it impossible for one to respond to the grace of God. To those who do not respond, God sends a great delusion.

The good news is that God loves you and offers you eternal life. All that you need to do is receive His gift. Today is the day of your salvation.

1. We see that God does not reprimand the martyred saints for asking Him to avenge their deaths. What does Scripture say about vengeance?

Leviticus 19:18

Deuteronomy 32:35

2 Samuel 22:48

Nahum 1:2

Hebrews 10:30

2. Why must we leave vengeance to God?

3. How can we be sure that all of the evil that will happen is clearly in God's control and plan?

Proverbs 19:21


Job 42:2


Isaiah 46:10-13


Isaiah 14:24-27


4. Why must God bring judgment to the earth?


5. After all the evil that is unleashed in these judgments, the survivors are still unrepentant. How can this be explained?

6. Materialism and the works of their hands become the objects of worship. What exactly were they worshiping? Be specific.

7. Do you see this same type of worship going on today?

8. What does it mean to worship an idol? What is an idol?

9. Why would demon worship and idolatry be linked together?

10. List the four sins that will be prevalent in this Great Tribulation.

11. As you look at the world in which you live, do you see any similarities and/or differences in the lifestyles of people today compared with those who will live in the time of the Tribulation? Do you think this is significant? Discuss.

The Euphrates River . . . was the place where sin was first known, where misery first began, where the first lie was told, where the first murder was committed, where the first grave was dug. The Euphrates River was the scene of the rise of Israel's greatest and most oppressive enemies. The Euphrates River was the scene of the two great apostasies before and after the Flood. The Euphrates River was the scene of the long years in which the children of Israel dragged out the wearisome days of their captivity. The Euphrates River was the scene of the rise of those great world empires that oppressed civilization in the ancient day, cruel Persians and the Medes . . ."[3]

[1] John Walvoord, *The Revelation of Jesus Christ* (Chicago: Moody Press, 1966), 99.

[2] Joseph Seiss, *The Apocalypse* (Grand Rapids: Zondervan, 1964)

[3] Criswell, *Expository Sermons on Revelation* (Grand Rapids: Zondervan, 1962), 190.

# Divine Parenthesis

In this lesson we want to examine the messenger that descends from heaven and the message he brings.

OUTLINE  R E V E L A T I O N   1 0 : 1 - 1 1

We might think from the progress and development of evil that Satan is going to preside over this earth forever. But this divine parenthesis reminds us that God is still Sovereign Lord, that He has not forgotten His own, and that ultimately they will be victorious.

  I. **The Messenger from Heaven** • Revelation 10:1-3a
  A. The descent of this messenger from heaven
  B. The description of this messenger from heaven
  C. The deeds of this messenger from heaven
 II. **The Message from Heaven** • Revelation 10:3b-7
  A. A seven-fold message
  B. A sealed-up message
  C. A sworn message
III. **The Mandate from Heaven** • Revelation 10:8-11

One of the fundamental characteristics and attributes of God is His mercy. Throughout the history of man, even in his darkest days of rebellion and sin, he has been wooed by a loving God. Against the darkest backdrop of iniquity, God has painted in brilliant tones His love and kindness. Nowhere in the Bible is that more beautifully pictured than here in the Apocalypse.

As we begin the 10th chapter, we are entering an interlude, or a parenthesis, in the action. When we use a parenthesis, it usually denotes information that does not carry on the flow of the argument but is nonetheless necessary information for the reader to have. Revelation 10: 1-11: 14 forms an interlude, or parenthesis, between the blowing of the sixth and seventh trumpets. In these chapters we are told of three special words of testimony and witness from God. The first is from a mighty angel (Revelation 10: 1-11), the second from two special witnesses (Revelation 11: 1-14), and the third from the elders in heaven (vv. 15-19). However depressing the events of a time might seem, God is not without His witness.

Even though the ultimate triumph of Christ does not occur until after the pouring out of the seventh bowl, the Spirit of God conveys John ahead in time to show him a vignette of this triumph over the earth. With the heaviness of what has gone before, this is relief, hope, and assurance for every child of God. This vision has been heralded by critics as the most magnificent, glorious picture in all the annals of history. It cannot be rivaled in terms of its picturesque prose. As we examine the text, note how each part of this vision is completely unique.

## The Messenger from Heaven

Into John's consciousness comes the picture of a messenger who has come down from heaven to bring a message of encouragement and hope to John, and to all the believers of his day.

## The Descent of This Messenger from Heaven

It is important to know that this is not a fallen angel. This angel descends out of heaven at the will of God. He is not said to have fallen down or to have been thrown down. This is not the first time we have met this angel. He has appeared in this book twice before. In chapter 7 he holds back the judgments that are about to fall as God performs a special work of grace. In chapter 8 he appears again as the messenger of the covenant, pouring out fire and judgment upon the earth. Here in chapter 10 he appears as king, taking back possession of the earth. So we see him as prophet, prince, and king.

Who is this angel? There is much controversy over his identity. Some say he is Michael; others say he is a special archangel appointed by God to fulfill certain functions. But the description given to him will not allow for such a misunderstanding. This is the Angel of Jehovah, the Lord Himself. The Lord often came to His people in the Old Testament as the Angel of Jehovah. The Angel of Jehovah is the preincarnate Christ. He is a special personage for the Jews. We know that God has programmed history around His people and that the first 69 weeks (as the term is used in the book of Daniel) has to do with the Jewish nation. Between the 69th and 70th weeks there is a parenthesis of grace. This is the period known as the church age. But in this 10th chapter we are no longer in the age of grace, but we are in the 70th week of Daniel, which is again Jewish in its origin. Therefore, we should not be surprised that the Lord appears here in the same way He did in the Old Testament. To substantiate this position further we need only look at how this messenger is described.

## The Description of This Messenger from Heaven

The first description we are given about this messenger is that he is clothed with a cloud. Clouds have always been associated with the presence of God. On Mount Sinai, the Lord descended in a thick cloud (Exodus 19:9). God led Israel by a cloud (Exodus 16:10). A cloud received Jesus when He ascended to heaven (Acts 1:9). When Jesus comes back, it will be in the clouds (Revelation 1:7). This surely identifies the mighty angel as the Lord Jehovah.

Next, we are told a rainbow was on his head. The rainbow has always been associated with God's promise to Noah not to destroy the earth again by water (Genesis 9:13). In Revelation, the rainbow again is an assuring promise from God that there is mercy in His judgment (Revelation 4:2-3). He assures His people that He has not forgotten them.

This messenger is said to be covered in glory, and this can only be descriptive of the Lord. We saw His glory in the

Transfiguration (Matthew 17:2), Paul's conversion (Acts 26:13), and in Malachi 4:2, where Jesus is referred to as the Sun of Righteousness.

The last description tells us he is carried on feet like pillars of fire. We saw a similar description in Revelation 1:15.

## The Deeds of This Messenger from Heaven

The book that he is holding is the same as that described in Revelation 5:5. This time however, the book is opened, and it is unsealed. All the judgments have been released and the Lord holds the open book as proof that His wrath has been fulfilled. By standing on the sea and on land, the Lord is reminding us that He is still in control of the earth, that the earth is His possession. He is said to have cried with a loud voice as a lion. Proverbs 19:12 says the king's wrath is like the roaring of a lion. Joel also refers to the Lord's voice as a roar (Joel 3:16).

## The Message from Heaven

As the One who comes from heaven roars, there is a seven gun salute (so to speak) from heaven.

## A Seven-Fold Message

As the angel roars like a lion, his voice is accompanied by a seven-fold thunder from heaven. Often in the Bible, the voice of the Lord's judgment is compared to thunder (Job 26:14). Psalm 29 is a wonderful commentary on the seven thunders of Revelation 10. If we read through the psalm we discover that the "voice of the Lord" thunders exactly seven times. The voice of the Lord is powerful, is full of majesty, breaks the cedars, divides the flames of fire, shakes the wilderness, makes the deer give birth, and strips the forests bare.

## A Sealed-Up Message

This message from heaven is indeed a strange one. This is the first and only time in this book that John is forbidden to reveal the content of the revelation that he receives. The message of the seven thunders is not to be communicated. Daniel had a similar instruction given to him (Daniel 12:8-9). This brief message in the thunders is the only hidden revelation that the entire book contains. John had been told to "write everything he had seen, the things that were, and that would be"

(Revelation 1:19). Also at the end of the book (Revelation 22:10), there is a reminder that the information is not to be hidden. Since we are not told what information the seven thunders contain, many have tried to delve into their meaning. Vikings interpreted them as the seven Crusades; Danbuz made them the seven nations that received the Reformation; Elliott makes them the Pope's bull against Luther; and, Seventh-day Adventism has presumed to reveal the things which were uttered. We need to remember that "The secret things belong to the Lord our God . . ." (Deuteronomy 29: 29). What God has commanded sealed is not for us to know.

## A Sworn Message

After the sound of the seven thunders, the mighty angel lifted up his hand and swore by the Eternal Creator that there should no longer be any delay. The cup of human iniquity was full. Many have tried to use this action to disqualify him as the Angel of Jehovah. How could God lift up His hand to swear by God? But if we study Hebrews 6:13,17-18, we see God making a promise to Abraham. Because He could swear by no one greater, He swore by Himself. What oath was this messenger making? "That there should be delay no longer" (Revelation 10:6e). The word for time in this phrase is the word *chronos*. This expression "there shall be time no longer" is not an oath that ends time as we know it, but that time has run out. Surely this announcement is an answer to the prayers of the souls of them that were slain for the Word of God (Revelation 6:9-10).

We have been told that there will be no more delay, that judgment will begin and be fulfilled. But what will happen when this judgment ends? "The mystery of God would be finished" (Revelation 10:7). The obvious question this statement raises is centered around the identification of this mystery. Some say it is the mystery of the completion of the church. But that happened in the prophetic scheme long ago. William R. Newell offers this possibility: " . . . all those counsels and dealings of God made known by Him to and through the Old Testament prophets, concerning His governmental proceedings with men on earth, looking always toward the establishment of the kingdom in the hands of Christ." Newell is probably right in the broad scope of this answer, but we can be more specific.

I believe the mystery that will be revealed at the end of the Tribulation is the mystery of the silence of heaven. For centuries God has remained silent and there have been very few interventions of divine judgment. Sin has seemed to go unchecked and evil has been unbridled. But here in this end time, at this last moment, the mystery will be finished.

## The Mandate from Heaven

This is the first time that John has been asked to take upon himself the role of an actor in the drama of the Apocalypse. He is asked to eat the book which is in the angel's hand. Godet says this command to eat "represents the most complete spiritual assimilation. This nourishment is to strengthen him for taking up again the great prophecy relating to all the peoples and nations and tongues and kings." This book listed all of the judgments that would be poured out upon the world. When John was told to eat that book, it was a command to assimilate the truth of that prophecy and be ready to go to the nations with a warning. Before John could preach the judgment of God, he had to be identified with God in His judgment. God's word was to literally become a part of him. This is the kind of spiritual involvement that all preachers should have with their text before they open their mouths to declare God's truth.

John was warned by the angel that the book would be sweet to the taste but bitter in his belly. If John assimilates the book, he will have the feelings of judgment in his stomach. There will be joy in preaching God's truth but sorrow in contemplating the rejection of that truth by those who hear. Preaching prophetic truth is a bittersweet experience.

Any true preacher of the Bible will find himself identifying with these two emotions often. If the sweet is not mixed with the bitter, a congregation will likely die from discouragement. But if only the sweet is preached and the bitter judgment to come is never taught, that congregation is likely to spend eternity in hell.

1. How can you know this messenger was not an ordinary angel, but the Angel of Jehovah?

2. Compare the description of the Angel of Jehovah with that of the "Son of Man" in Revelation 1:13-16.

3. Give the significance of each element of this messenger's appearance.

Clothed with a cloud.

A rainbow on his head.

Covered with glory.

Feet like pillars of fire.

4. Why does this messenger carry an open book?

5. Who was it that opened this book? Does this answer give you more proof that this messenger was indeed the Angel of Jehovah?

6. Why does this angel stand on the sea and on the land?

7. Since God was not going to allow John to reveal the sealed-up message, why do you think it is even included in Scripture?

8. Do you find yourself asking questions similar to those of the slain saints in Revelation 6:10? Who else asked similar questions?

Psalm 73:3-16

Psalm 94:3-7

Jeremiah 12:1-2


9. What answers does Scripture give us about the wicked and our attitude toward them?

Psalm 37

Psalm 73:17-22

Psalm 94:8-23

Deuteronomy 32:35-36

Romans 12:19


10. Why was John given instructions to eat the little book?

11. What is a believer's responsibility to the Word of God?

2 Timothy 2:15

1 Peter 3:15

2 Timothy 4:2


DID YOU KNOW?

The Angel of Jehovah had feet like pillars of fire. This was significant because we see fire being used as a symbol of judgment and testing in the Bible.

# The Two Witnesses

In this lesson we will study the two witnesses God sends to prophesy for three and one-half years. We will consider their identity, their ministry and their ministry's effects.

OUTLINE R E V E L A T I O N   1 1 : 1 - 1 4

Something very dramatic has taken place between chapters 3 and 4, and the Rapture is the only possible explanation for the shift in emphasis. We will examine the reasons for this conclusion and John's vision of heaven with the throne as its focus of worship.

I. **Principles for Understanding** • Revelation 11
   A. It is Jewish in nature
   B. It is prophetic
   C. Interpret it literally
   D. Consider its setting
II. **The Two Witnesses** • Revelation 11:3-12
   A. They are people
   B. They are prophets
      1. The argument for Elijah
      2. The argument for Moses
   C. They are powerful
   D. They are persecuted
   E. They are preserved
III. **The Earthquake** • Revelation 11:13

Many scholars have labeled the 11th chapter of the Book of Revelation as one of the most difficult chapters in the Bible to interpret. However, I believe there are three essential underlying presuppositions that make this passage understandable, and if we keep these in mind we won't get lost in our discussion.

### Its Jewish Nature

We can see that the discussion in this chapter centers not on the church, but on a time in the future when the Jews will be back in the center of God's plan. This is evident in the references to the Holy City, the temple, and the furniture of the temple.

### It Is Prophetic

This chapter is not to be understood historically. Remember: At the time John is writing there is no temple in existence. The temple had been destroyed. This chapter anticipates a time in the future.

### Interpret It Literally

We get into trouble when we allegorize and symbolize passages that should be taken literally. The great city referred to here is Jerusalem; the time periods are actual days and months; the two witnesses are actual people; the earthquake is real; the seven thousand men who die are real men; the resurrection of the two witnesses actually will occur.

### The Setting

Remember that chapter 11 is a continuation of chapter 10. There is no serious break in thought. We are still in the interlude that began in chapter 10.

The first two verses in chapter 11 give us the location for the events that will follow. The first action we see is a command to measure the temple of God. If you do a survey of the Bible, you will find that there are five temples mentioned in Scripture. The first is Solomon's temple that was destroyed by Nebuchadnezzar in 587 B.C. (2 Chronicles 36:13-21). The second temple was built by Zerubbabel when he brought the captives back from Babylon (Ezra 5:2). It was destroyed in 168 B.C. by Antiochus Epiphanes. The third temple was known as Herod's temple and was destroyed by Titus in A.D. 70. The last two temples are yet to be built. They are the Tribulation temple (which is the next to be built) and the millenary temple that Ezekiel talks about in his prophecy (Ezekiel 40-44).

The temple mentioned in chapter 11 is the temple the Israelites will build as they are regathered in Israel. We must realize that the Jews are not going back to Israel in belief. It is not a spiritual movement as many think. The temple to be built during the Tribulation is not due to a spiritual awakening. Instead, this temple will house the headquarters for the Antichrist (2 Thessalonians 2:3-4).

The Antichrist will make a covenant with the Jews in order to form an alliance with them. He will promise to help them build a temple so they can worship according to their customs. But in the middle of the Tribulation, the Antichrist will break his covenant and desecrate the temple. This is known as the Abomination of Desolation.

In the first verse of chapter 11, John is asked to measure the temple with a rod. We know this instruction has nothing to do with validating the measurements of the temple. God is telling John that this Jewish court will be judged. Remember that every time the word "rod" is used in the Book of Revelation it has to do with judgment.

### The Two Witnesses

In verse three we are introduced to the two witnesses. There is much debate as to when these witnesses will appear on the scene. I believe they begin their ministry at the beginning of the Tribulation, at the time the Antichrist makes his covenant with the Jewish people. Some believe the two witnesses are the means whereby the 144,000 will be sealed as preachers unto righteousness. We can assume they will have a great following.

What do we know about these witnesses? There are five areas we need to look at:

THEY ARE PEOPLE—They are not the Old and New Testament, nor are they the law and the prophets. They are real people. We are told that their dead bodies will lie in the street for three and one-half days. They are also described as wearing sackcloth. Sackcloth is presented in Scripture as an outward expression of mourning or repentance. Jacob put on sackcloth when he heard of Joseph's "death" (Genesis 37:34), and David mourned Abner's death by dressing in sackcloth (2 Samuel 3:31).

In Revelation 11:4 these two witnesses are called "two olive trees and two lampstands standing before the Lord of the earth." How can these two descriptions help us determine that the witnesses are real people? If we look at the prophecy of Zechariah we see, again, two witnesses: Joshua and Zerubbabel (Zechariah 4:1-14). God uses the lampstand and the olive tree as a picture of them. The lampstand burned brightly and the olive tree produced the oil, which was burned in the candelabra. It is a picture of the fact that these two witnesses are going to shine in the darkness of the Tribulation and that they will be fueled by the holy oil of the Spirit of God.

THEY ARE PROPHETS—One commentator described them as "Jesus freaks" out there telling everybody what is going to happen. They will prophesy. It is interesting to note that God sends two of them. Think through the Bible of how God dispatches in twos.

The question that has really caused debate and speculation over the years is centered around the identity of the two witnesses. Many scholars believe one to be Elijah the prophet, reincarnated. If we look at Malachi 3:1-3 and 4:5-6, we are told that Elijah will come before Jesus returns. This prophecy is fulfilled in Revelation, chapter 11. It is also interesting to note that at the passover the Jewish people set a cup on the table and call it Elijah's cup. They do this because every Orthodox Jew knows this passage of prophecy. They know that before the Messiah comes Elijah must come first. Some commentators say that John the Baptist was the fulfillment of the Malachi prophecy. This is impossible because John was asked if he were Elijah, and he said no (John 1: 21).

Another reason I believe it to be Elijah is because Elijah didn't die. Elijah was taken to heaven in a whirlwind of fire. Elijah also uses the same sign in the Tribulation as he used when he was a prophet. In 1 Kings 17 Elijah stopped the rain, and in Revelation 11:6 he is seen to "have power to shut heaven so that no rain falls in the days of their prophecy." It is also significant that Elijah appeared with Moses in the Transfiguration.

If Elijah is the first witness, who is the second? I believe it to be Moses for these reasons: Moses and Elijah had already been paired together at the Transfiguration. Moses performed the second half of the miracles where we see Elijah performing the first. For example, Elijah shut heaven and Moses turned the rivers to blood. Moses died, but no one knows where his body is buried (Deuteronomy 34:5-6). The body of Moses was preserved by God so that he might be restored. In the Jewish culture, the law and the prophets are understood. Moses is the law and Elijah is the prophet.

We must keep in mind that it is impossible to prove conclusively who these two witnesses are. We have strong evidence to support the belief that they are Moses and Elijah. But if they are not these two men, we can know that they are very much like them and have the same kind of ministry.

THEY ARE POWERFUL—These witnesses are given unbelievable power by God. The corruption of that day is so overwhelming that their preaching causes the masses to hate them. Picture the scene. Into a godless society come two men dressed in sackcloth, preaching about Christ who is Lord of all the earth. They shut the heavens so no rain will fall during their ministry, and they have power to cause plagues as often as they desire. They go about testifying of the wickedness of the people. They tell the people that God has been responsible for all the judgments that have been poured out. If that is not enough, they will tell them of more terrifying judgments to come. They preach against the Beast of Revelation 13 and anger the Jews by telling them their worship in the temple is pure paganism. Men try to destroy them because their witness exposes the wickedness of the earth. But God has provided them with protection. Revelation 11:5 says, "If anyone wants to harm them, fire proceeds from their mouth and devours their enemies." These witnesses will have power over death, drought, and disease.

THEY ARE PERSECUTED—God gives the two witnesses 42 months to accomplish their ministry. They cannot be killed until their testimony is finished, until God gives His permission. They will be killed by the Beast who ascends from the bottomless pit. The two witnesses are so hated that the entire world will rejoice at their deaths. Their bodies will be put on public display. Verses 8 and 9 tell us that their bodies will lie in the street for three and one-half days. In Biblical Jewish society this was an abomination. Even the worst criminals were afforded burial with some dignity. In their culture a person was buried on the very day of his death (unless there was an embalming procedure and he lay in state). These two men will have engendered such hatred that they will be left in the center of the city—on public display in the hot sun for all the eyes of the world to watch.

Notice the delight of their enemies. Verse 10 tells us "they will rejoice over them, make merry, and send gifts to one another, because these two prophets tormented those who dwell on the earth." They will be ecstatic that someone has finally put an end to these two nemeses who were driving them crazy with their preaching. One writer describes the scene like this: "Now comes the real revelation of the heart of man; glee, horrid insane inhuman hellish ghoulish glee. There is actual delight at the death of God's witnesses—utter unbounded delight." Newspapers will have entire front pages of jubilation. Excursions will be taken into Jerusalem so as to see the unburied corpses of the prophets of God. It will be a festival, a holiday, a regular "Christmastime of hell" that ensues. It is hard to believe how angry righteous men can make unrighteous men. But when a preacher preaches the truth about judgment, he makes people so mad that they rejoice when he is killed.

THEY ARE PRESERVED—We may ask the question: Why will this awful scene have to take place? This transpires so the whole world will validate their deaths. They are already decomposing, and the next action we see is that they stand up! The whole world will see this. Remember the world is looking in on this scene. It is on the news and in the papers, the focus of world attention for the last three and one-half days. They are not only resurrected; they are raptured (v. 12). They go up into heaven in "a cloud." This cloud is the *shekinah* glory of God. It is the same cloud that the angel of chapter 10 was clothed in.

### The Earthquake

At the hour of their ascension there will be a great earthquake. As a result of this quake, one-tenth of the city will fall, 7,000 men will be killed, and the rest of the people will be terrified and give glory to God. During the Tribulation there will be such a class system that people will gravitate around those in position who have something to offer. Those are the 7,000 men the earthquake kills. It won't be accidental, and it won't be misunderstood. People will realize this was not a random judgment.

We now see great joy turning into great fear. In verse 13 we are told that "the rest were afraid and gave glory to the God of heaven." This sounds as if they will finally turn from their wicked ways and turn to God. But this will be due to fear, not faith. They do not turn to God in repentance but in a temporary state of awe and fear that brings forth a terrifying call upon the Lord. If we look in the next chapter, we see that they will still be rebellious and hardened against God.

The question we need to ask ourselves is: Where are we? God sends events in our lives to get our attention. When the pain goes away, what do we do? Do we walk away from God? The Book of Revelation reminds us that God's grace will end. But even during the time of judgment God extends His grace. The two witnesses preaching for three and one-half years exemplify this. God's day of grace will not go on forever. If He has been talking to you, today is the day to respond. His Spirit will not strive with you forever!

## APPLICATION REVELATION 11:1-14

1. What principles do you need to keep in mind to interpret this chapter?

2. Why is John given a rod to measure the temple?

3. Since Herod's temple was destroyed in A.D. 70, what temple is John to measure?

4. Describe the condition of the people of the Tribulation.

5. What clues are given in our passage to validate the fact that the two witnesses are real people?

6. Revelation 11:4 describes the witnesses as lampstands and olive trees. Using Zechariah 4:1-14, relate how these two phrases add proof to the argument that the witnesses are real people.

7. What is the ministry of the two witnesses?

8. Do you agree that the two witnesses are Elijah and Moses? Why, or why not?

9. How are these two men going to protect themselves against such a hostile people?



10. Why are they hated?


11. Who kills the two witnesses?


12. Why do their bodies lie in the street for three and one-half days?


13. Describe the scene after their death as best you can imagine it.




14. What will be the reaction of the people when the two witnesses are resurrected?




15. In verse 13 we are told that the people give glory to God. Will a great revival take place? Defend your answer.

16. What have you learned about God's grace and judgment?

DID YOU KNOW:

Antiochus Epiphanes considered himself Zeus and encouraged people to worship him. He attacked the Jews on their Sabbath and burned and plundered their city. He determined to destroy the Jewish religion. He forbid them to live in accordance with their laws and customs. He destroyed copies of the Torah and ordered idolatrous altars set up. Disobedience meant death. His most famous deed was making the temple the place of worship of Olympian Zeus and offering swine flesh on the altar. His actions sparked the Maccabean revolution.